PROMOTING
GOOD PROGRESS
IN PRIMARY SCHOOLS

Sara Miller McCune founded Sage Publishing in 1965 to support the dissemination of useable knowledge and educate a global community. Sage publishes more than 1000 journals and over 800 new books each year, spanning a wide range of subject areas. Our growing selection of library products includes archives, data, case studies and video. Sage remains majority owned by our founder and after her lifetime will become owned by a charitable trust that secures the company's continued independence.

Los Angeles | London | New Delhi | Singapore | Washington DC | Melbourne

PROMOTING
GOOD PROGRESS
IN PRIMARY SCHOOLS

CAROLINE WHITING
PAUL RICHARDSON

Learning Matters
A Sage Publishing Company
1 Oliver's Yard
55 City Road
London EC1Y 1SP

Sage Publications Inc.
2455 Teller Road
Thousand Oaks, California 91320

Sage Publications India Pvt Ltd
B 1/I 1 Mohan Cooperative Industrial Area
Mathura Road
New Delhi 110 044

Sage Publications Asia-Pacific Pte Ltd
3 Church Street
#10-04 Samsung Hub
Singapore 049483

First published in 2024

Library of Congress Number Available

British Library Cataloguing in Publication Data

A catalogue record for this book is available from the British Library

Editor: Amy Thornton
Senior project editor: Chris Marke
Project management: TNQ Tech Pvt. Ltd.
Cover design: Wendy Scott
Typeset by: TNQ Tech Pvt. Ltd.
Printed in the UK

ISBN 978-1-5296-7245-9
ISBN 978-1-5296-7244-2 (pbk)

CONTENTS

ABOUT THE AUTHORS

Paul Richardson was formerly a Senior Lecturer on the primary PGCE at Bath Spa University and was co-lead for the English team with Caroline Whiting. He is now an Assistant Professor on the educational equity (Malaysia) course at University of Birmingham. His interests are in rural primary schools and multi-academy trusts which were part of his doctoral research. He has external examiner experience on iQTS courses and moderating AOQTS routes. His research interests include teacher's perceptions of writing including student teacher's anxiety in teaching writing and exploring the impact of prescriptive schemes in schools on teacher professionalism.

Caroline Whiting has been a Senior Lecturer on the primary PGCE at Bath Spa University for nearly ten years and co-leads the English team, with Paul Richardson until December 2023. Other key interests within the programme are planning and assessment. She has external examining experience with three other universities, including international PGCE programmes, and supervises postgraduate research. She has taught in primary, middle and secondary schools, and was a primary head teacher before becoming a school improvement adviser and Newly Qualified Teacher (NQT) co-ordinator with the local authority. She has maintained a keen research interest in Initial Teacher Training since her PhD thesis on school-based training and has been involved in two large-scale national projects, producing 'topographies' of the current ITT landscape. Recent projects together with Paul Richardson have included PGCE students' perceptions of learning to teach English, especially writing, writing anxiety and the impact of schemes of work or commercial programmes on teachers' planning capacity, and their professional autonomy.

INTRODUCTION

When we discuss the purpose of education for both now, and for the future, the language we tend to use gives the *'impression that education is monolithic, i.e., that it is one thing with only one aim'* (Biesta, 2019 p.13). Biesta identifies three important functions of education: qualification, socialisation and subjectification. Qualification, where children and young people are qualified to do certain things, includes the acquisition of knowledge, skills and dispositions that children are anticipated to learn to perform specific roles and function in modern society. Biesta states that this function tends to be aligned with more conservative perspectives towards education that encourage a more 'back to basics' emphasis within a curriculum.

Socialisation is another function of education that can be understood as children taking part in cultural, social traditions and practices. Again, Biesta (2019) argues that a narrow interpretation of this function can be focused on picking up the ways of doing and being of a particular job or profession. 'Socialisation is, in other words, about becoming part of certain ways of doing, both informal and formal and institution-alised' (Biesta, 2019 p.14). In part 3, when we look at the Early Years and Primary curricula, we can observe a shift in focus. The Early Years curriculum places greater emphasis on socialisation within children's learning, whereas in children progress through key stage 1 and 2 there is arguably a greater focus on qualifications over socialisation.

Biesta (2017) argues that functionalist or instrumentalist views of education reduce the teacher's role to being the deliverer of the curriculum. This reductionist perspective erodes the sense of autonomy and empowerment that comes with being a teacher. From a policy level, Biesta (2015) states that teachers can tend to be seen as 'factors' that can be tweaked so they work in the most effective and efficient way as possible, which will consequently lead to an increase in performance of the educational system (p.75). But rather than teachers being reduced/interpreted/perceived as technicians or craft workers, they can be informed professionals (Orchard and Winch, 2015). Wood (2011) argues that everyday life in classrooms is fundamentally affected by political beliefs and actions, and this is why in this book we want to ensure you, the reader, approach what might be a seemingly obvious or commonsense is in fact influenced, or politically driven, particularly if it is argued/perceived to be the 'correct' way to do it (ibid). Thus, para-phrasing Biesta (2017), it is important that beginning teachers understand that their intellectual freedom as professional teachers is more than how to deliver a curriculum; it is also about being autonomous and critically informed professionals.

As a beginning teacher, during induction, and in subsequent posts, you will always be subject to frame-works, policies and other constraints of one sort or another. These come from government, school inspection, academy trusts, individual or groups of schools, even private companies that provide teaching schemes and assessments. Teachers cannot simply do as they like. There can be good reasons for this, as long as they are applied thoughtfully, knowledgeably and critically. Shared understandings, systems and processes, working with a common language and common aims, can support us in working effectively together, providing an entitlement to learning and progress for every child. One of the purposes of this book is to help you make sense of the current context, at the same time as supporting you in your practice, to the benefit of the children in your charge. To this end, after setting out some theoretical lenses through which to think about progress, and the historical and current national contexts which frame current practice, we explore the detail of both statutory and guidance documents, identifying key elements that can be effective in developing our ideas around pupil progress. These include national curricula, training and development frameworks for initial teacher training and induction, teachers' standards and inspection. The sections that detail both school-wide and day-to-day practices in school, helping you to develop and refine your own practice, are set firmly within the policy documents of the day, but are also designed to support your critical thinking, especially through the reflective questions. This is something you can take forward in your career, helping you to negotiate the future as a primary school teacher, no matter the context.

PART 1
WHAT IS PROGRESS?

**LINKS TO THE CORE CONTENT FRAMEWORK
(CORE CONTENT AND EARLY CAREER FRAMEWORK)**

Standard 1 – 'Set high expectations'

1.2. Teachers are key role models, who can influence the attitudes, values and behaviours of their pupils.

1.3. Teacher expectations can affect pupil outcomes; setting goals that challenge and stretch pupils *(from their starting point)* is essential.

Standard 2 – 'Promote good progress'

2.1. Learning involves a lasting change in pupils' capabilities or understanding.

Standard 3 – 'Demonstrate good subject and curriculum knowledge'

3.1. A school's curriculum enables it to set out its vision for the knowledge, skills and values that its pupils will learn, encompassing the national curriculum within a coherent wider vision for successful learning.

Standard 4 – 'Plan and teach well structured lessons'

4.1. Effective teaching can transform pupils' knowledge, capabilities and beliefs about learning.

Standard 5 – 'Adapt teaching'

5.2 *(5.3)*. Seeking to understand pupils' differences, including their different levels of prior knowledge and potential barriers to learning, is an essential part of teaching.

Standard 6 – 'Make accurate and productive use of assessment'

6.1. Effective assessment is critical to teaching because it provides teachers with information about pupils' understanding and needs.

6.3. Before using any assessment, teachers should be clear about the decision it will be used to support and be able to justify its use.

Standard 7 – 'Manage behaviour effectively'

7.7. Pupils' investment in learning is also driven by their prior experiences and perceptions of success and failure.

Standard 8 – 'Fulfil wider professional responsibilities'

8.2. Reflective practice, supported by feedback from and observation of experienced colleagues, professional debate and learning from educational research, is also likely to support improvement.

1
DIFFERENT WAYS OF UNDERSTANDING PROGRESS

KEY WORDS: ASSESSMENT; CURRICULUM; KNOWLEDGE; LEARNING

KNOWLEDGE AND VALUE – THE IDEAL PUPIL PRODUCT

Progress ranks with education and science as three of the most used and abused words in our contemporary vocabulary.

(Bossard, 1931)

On the surface, the term 'progress' may seem clear and incontrovertible. It is a term frequently used in schools, by the government and by other individuals or organisations involved in primary education. The Oxford English Dictionary defines progress (noun) as the '[o]nward movement following a prescribed course, in a specific direction, or towards a particular place' (OED, 2023). Or, in its verb form, progress is defined as '[t]o go or move forward or onward in space; to proceed, advance (through or along some course, path, etc.)'. Progress, therefore, is understood to be movement between points or, more precisely, an advancement, from one point to another, often following a specific course or path. How does this definition apply to the context of primary education? What are these 'points' and how do we move between them? And how do we know which path or direction we are supposed to be moving towards?

In seeking answers to these questions, we will try to clarify the idea, and use, of the term 'progress' in primary education. It will hopefully become clearer that the concept of progress is particularly obscured by its association with other elements within primary education, primarily knowledge, curriculum, learning and assessment. Additionally, as we explore the concept of progress together, we will see how our understanding of this term does not exist in isolation but is in fact framed and influenced by our assumptions regarding knowledge, curriculum, learning and assessment. This is why is it important to briefly unpick these concepts and a few of the assumptions behind them; in particular, how our own assumptions may have influenced our own understanding of and use of the term 'progress' and other associated terms with this concept.

The Office for Standards in Education, Children's Services and Skills (Ofsted) defines 'progress' as '*knowing more (including knowing how to do more) and remembering more*' (Ofsted, 2019a p.4). Ofsted do clarify that 'progress' '*should not be defined primarily by meeting standards or hitting the next data point*'. Instead, they explain that '*learning the curriculum itself is progress*' and stipulate that if pupils are attaining '*within a well-sequenced, well-constructed curriculum, they are making progress*' (Ofsted, 2019a p.5). This description aligns well with this definition of progress shared at the beginning, of it being a movement that follows a prescribed course, or towards a particular place (OED, 2023). Ofsted interpretation of progress is very much situated within the discipline of cognitive psychology, which defines learning as an alteration in long-term memory. Cognitive psychology and cognitive neuroscience have had a significant impact on educational policy and practice within England. Evidence of this can be seen in the level of research done by the Education Endowment Fund and the increased presence of key concepts such as memory retrieval in the Core Curriculum Framework and Early Career Framework. Indeed, scientific terms such as retrieval practice, cognitive load and spaced learning have become part of the established lexicon in primary school settings and no doubt is something you have been exposed to in your career as a teacher.

There are those such as Professor Claxton (2021) who oppose the idea that learning, and consequently progress, can be reduced to 'knowing more' and 'remembering more'. He argued that drilling facts and formulae into long-term memory works quite well for some limited types of learning, but we need to be careful. Otherwise, knowledge can end up being reduced to 'facts' and 'subject content' which children are then tested on further down the line. This reductive view towards learning, argues Claxton, ignores significant learning that helps children to take penalty kicks, empower and enable them to tell entertaining stories, support children's appreciation of artists such as Matisse or understand the complexities of climate change. Claxton (2021) explains that children cannot learn to do these things by merely learning about them or by being told and tested. He argues that they need to listen, read, remember, rehearse and reproduce.

Additionally, Nuthall (2001) raised concerns regarding any reductive perception of knowledge, and subsequently progress, which carries the position that both learning and consequently progress can be reduced to numerical values. The attraction of this approach is that it enables, and encourages, comparisons to be made between individual child and their peers. Further still, this reductive approach carries the assumption that progress can still be measured in a meaningful and accurate way (Selfridge, 2019) that benefits children. As we further explore this later in the book, it will become apparent that this emphasis on reducing progress to numerical values becomes less about informing and improving teaching and learning, and instead more about holding schools and teachers to account (Selfridge, 2019). Due to performativity (Ball, 2023) and established accountability measures within education, such as school league tables, there is a vested invest in ensuring this numerical-based approach is maintained within education.

Selfridge (2019) argues that systems that rely on this reductive approach, particularly national assessment systems, have a powerful sense of self-assured certainty in the use of numerical values to denote progress. Alarmed by this self-assuredness, Selfridge poses the question, 'what if comparing an individual child's progress with another is in fact a complete fallacy?' This question targets the held assumption that accurate (and fair) comparisons can be made between similarly aged children and can do so without including significant factors such as the children's social, economic and geographical backgrounds and experiences. Selfridge recognises how these factors can have a considerable influence on children's learning and progress, as we will come to see later in the book though it might not be in the way that you anticipate or presume. Nutall (2001) and Selfridge (2019) share concerns that numerically measurable progress will be assumed to be most valuable, or worst still, will be considered the only valid option in recognising progress in education.

THE RELATIONSHIP BETWEEN PROGRESS AND OTHER KEY CONCEPTS

In exploring our understanding of 'progress', we will come to see that this concept is inextricably linked to certain crucial terms within education, principally, curriculum, knowledge, learning and assessment. All of these play a vital role when considering and discussing the concept of progress. We have provided a diagram to help illustrate how these key terms relate to one another (see Figure 1.1). The three/four spokes of the 'progress wheel' are crucial in understanding and discussing progress in any educational setting. The first spoke is knowledge. Knowledge plays a key role because, from an instrumental perspective, knowledge makes up the constituent units or 'points' mentioned earlier in this chapter that children travel or progress along. Second is curriculum; this is the choosing and sequencing of knowledge that children will learn; in other words, the role of the curriculum is arguably to provide the designated/specific path that children follow. This is to ensure clarity and consistency on what should be measured to discern whether progress has taken place. The third is learning. Learning is considered the process with which enables or facilitates the advancement of progress. The last is assessment, which plays a crucial role in measuring and recognising the movement/advancement that has taken place and help signify whether 'progress' has occurred.

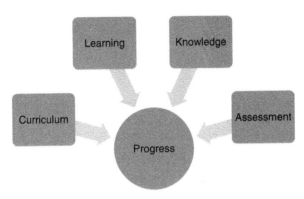

Figure 1.1   Key concepts

KNOWLEDGE

When the word 'knowledge' is used by others or yourself, how do you perceive this term? What do you believe qualifies as knowledge, and consequently, what does not qualify as knowledge? It is important to recognise how your own viewpoint towards knowledge is influenced by your experience of education, all of which contributes to and frames your beliefs towards knowledge and the purpose of education as well. This chapter will not be able to give justice to the enormous amount of literature on knowledge; the purpose is to encourage you to reflect on your own assumptions around knowledge, in particular what we regard as knowledge, and consequently what we might disregard as 'knowledge'. Currently, there is strong emphasis on the need to provide a 'knowledge-rich curriculum' in schools, to provide opportunities for all children and to ensure 'levelling up' occurs within schools (Gibb, 2021).

One major influence behind this increased emphasis on a 'knowledge-rich' curriculum in schools is the American educationalist and literary professor, E.D Hirsch (1988). He argued that the main purpose of education ought to be focused on ensuring children achieve social mobility, especially those children he considered were from disadvantaged backgrounds. The Organisation for Economic Co-operation and Development describe social mobility as a 'change in a person's socio-economic situation' so they can gain 'equality of opportunity', regardless of the socio-economic background of the individual, or because of their 'gender, age, sexual orientation, race, ethnicity, birthplace, or other *circumstances beyond their control'*. Hirsch (1988) claims that all children, particularly those from disadvantaged backgrounds, require a certain level of cultural literacy to achieve social mobility. Claxton (2021) states that this cultural literacy is often tied to the dominant (and privileged) culture within that society. This emphasis on ensuring all children gain this 'cultural literacy' can be seen in Gibb's assurance that the National Curriculum offers children the 'best that has been thought and said' (Gibb, 2021). Ofsted have expressed a similar point of view, evident in their definition of progress being *'knowing more'* and *'remembering more'* (Ofsted, 2019a p.4). They state that children need to be introduced to certain forms of 'essential knowledge', echoing word for word Gibb's sentiment above: 'the best that has been thought and said' (Ofsted, 2019b p.10).

In response to these calls for 'knowledge-rich' curricula, Claxton (2021) raises the issue of what type, or sort, of knowledge should be included within our curriculum? He explains that there are various forms of knowledge so *'we need to be clear about which forms of knowledge we want our schools to be rich in'* (Claxton, 2021 p.32). Additionally, Claxton advocates the teaching of skills and the inclusion of discussing these skills explicitly with children. He argues that this current 'knowledge-rich' approach is deliberately separating the teaching of skills and the teaching of 'knowledge' at opposite sides of the spectrum. One concept that links strongly with this idea of a 'knowledge-rich' curriculum is 'powerful knowledge'. The educationalist Michael Young (2014) advocated this idea of 'powerful knowledge'. He described it as (relatively) context-free knowledge, which offers opportunities for pupils at all ages to move beyond their own experience, to acquire knowledge that is not tied or bound by their experience. What is particularly attractive about the idea of powerful knowledge is the intended emphasis on children being introduced to new ways of thinking and subsequently being able to think about alternative futures (Young et al., 2014). So, children have power over their own knowledge and gain insight into what they can do to influence their own futures (Young et al., 2014).

Powerful knowledge and cultural literacy are considered to be important for those children who are recognised (and consequently labelled) as 'disadvantaged' as they *'may not have access to cultural capital, both in the home and then in their* school' (Ofsted, 2019b p.8). This 'cultural capital' is considered essential if children are to *'succeed in life'* and become *'educated citizens'* (Ofsted, 2019b p.10). Recent interpretations of this term used by organisations such as Ofsted are closer to Gramsci's (cited in Lears, 1985) idea of cultural hegemony. Cultural hegemony was the idea that most of the population within society consented to having preferred social values and norms imposed upon them by another more dominant and privileged group. This was accomplished through the dominant group's use of status and prestige within society which emphasises that certain 'culture literacies' are better to have over other cultural literacies, principally the cultural literacies of the privileged group which tends to be white middle class, in order to succeed in this society. Though this will be discussed further in chapter, it is important at this stage to recognise how this perspective inadvertently positions various cultural literacies, and cultural capital, into a hierarchical relationship. Evidence of this can be seen in the use of terms such as 'high' cultural capital, used by educationalists like Quigley (2022). It begs the question, 'what or, more importantly, who decides on what cultural capital is 'higher' than another?' Additionally, how does this emphasis on certain dominant cultural literacies over others influence educational policy, schools' institutional cultures and the personal experiences of children?

Another major influence on the concept of knowledge has been this idea of the 'knowledge economy', particularly people's perception of the purpose of education, and what should be taught in schools.

This idea places great emphasis on education being about preparing children for the job market, so schools should be focused on providing the skills, learning and knowledge to innovate to successfully participate in the economy (Ball, 2023). Moore and Young (2001) argue that as we have become a 'knowledge society', this will require more 'knowledge workers'. Thus, the expectation would be that children would need to learn '21st-century skills' to successfully thrive as citizens and workers in the 21st century (Partnership for 21st Century Skills cited in Biesta, 2019). Biesta (2019) argues that emphasis on the economy has been highly influential within educational policy, but it can result to a reductionist approach towards education which only favours literacy and mathematics, leading foundation subjects to be considered less essential. This way of interpreting knowledge, and the purpose of knowledge, is argued to be driven by economic imperatives which downplay the importance of 'powerful knowledge' which is believed to be required to critically engage with the world. This economic emphasis could lead, Biesta argues, towards a one-size-fits-all education that places intense pressure on teachers and schools to resolve the social and economic issues within society.

In response to his own question concerning which forms of knowledge we want our schools to be rich in, Claxton (2021) in his book *The Future of Teaching and the Myths That Hold It Back* has provided alternative perspective towards different forms of knowledge, included in the table below (Table 1.1).

Table 1.1   Forms of knowledge (Claxton, 2021 pp.32–33)

Type of knowledge	Description
Rote knowledge	Things you can retrieve and repeat, but which you may have no deep understanding of. Some of this may be useful, for example, learning your times tables by rote. Some of it may not be.
Factual knowledge	Isolated pieces of information that are taken as true.
Maxims	Rules of thumb that you know when and how to apply. Maxims are things you must remember to follow under specific circumstances, as guides to action. You can verbalise them, but they don't reflect states of the world; they tell you how to act.
Expertise – aka tacit, implicit or procedural knowledge	This is what philosophers call knowing how as opposed to knowing…as expertise becomes more subtle and nuanced, so the ability to articulate what you are doing becomes harder and harder.
Memories and impressions	Recollections of specific experiences. Memories present themselves to us as reliable records of our past, but we know only too well that a vivid memory and a strong feeling of 'having been there' are not always accurate. So, are memories and impressions strictly knowledge or not? And who is to say?
Feelings, emotions and intuitions	Being moved by a piece of music or a poem or having a hunch about the right way to proceed count as valid kinds of cognition.

Claxton (2021) argues that those who support a knowledge-rich curriculum are trying to re-create a traditional grammar school curriculum for all schools. Evidence of this approach can be seen in Nick Gibbs' speech to the Social Market Foundation panel event, where he states:

> Since 2010, the reforms that we put in place have been driven by the idea that the transmission of rich subject knowledge should be the priority for schools.

(Gibbs, 2021)

In doing this, Claxton's concern is that in creating these 'knowledge-rich' curricula, certain types of knowledge identified by Claxton such as memories, impressions, feelings and emotions will be classified as invaluable knowledge. What is deemed valuable or invaluable is also dependent on whether this knowledge can be reduced to measurable, numerical values and consequently can be tested. This leads to 'invaluable knowledge' having to compete with other types of knowledge that are considered far more valuable and may subsequently lead to the former being 'squeezed out of the classroom' (Claxton 2021).

CURRICULUM

Priestley (2019) explains how the concept of curriculum is often contested and misunderstood. Simply put, curriculum means a course of study. Priestley explains that word is derived from the Latin word meaning 'racecourse' or 'race' and has come to mean a general course which conveys the idea of going somewhere in a predefined direction. Priestley and Biesta (2013) claim that there is a close relationship between the two concepts knowledge and curriculum, because assumptions about the former contribute towards defining the structure of the latter.

Priestley (2019) does insist that the racecourse definition above does not sufficiently help us to understand the complex processes that take place in designing and implementing a curriculum. This is especially as the term 'curriculum' comes to mean different things to different people; additionally, the term 'curriculum' has a complex relationship with such concepts as pedagogy and assessment. Rather than being an objective and value-free process, Priestley (2019) believes that curriculum planning is fundamentally a political process because it involves and asserts certain values and (normative) judgements over other areas within education. For instance, Young (2014) states that curriculum can be considered the knowledge that children will acquire whilst at school, and pedagogy relates to the activities that teachers will prepare for these children to enable them to acquire this knowledge specified by the curriculum. From Young's point of view, these aspects are linked to one another, but are not influenced or dependent on the other. Priestley, on the other hand, claims that specific curriculum-planning models can exert a major influence on pedagogy:

> For instance, a framework that emphasises content to be learnt might encourage teacher-centred approaches to teaching, whereas a model based on processes and skills may encourage activities that are student-centred.

(Priestley, 2019)

Therefore, this and similar processes in education are not value free. Instead, we need to ask important questions regarding curricula such as 'Whose curriculum?' 'Who is it for and who chooses it?'

Some believe that content should be chosen to meet children's needs and/or interests. Others suggest that there are bodies of knowledge that have intrinsic value or help us access society's conversation, and which should be taught to all children. For instance, Young and Muller (2013) believe that children will be disadvantaged if they are not taught knowledge from the academic disciplines (which are recognised bodies of knowledge developed over generations by scholars using rigorous methods). Young (2014) argues that what distinguishes schools from other social institutions such as the family and work/business is that school's primary concern, 'as embodied in the specialist professional staff they recruit, and in their curriculum, is (or should be) to provide all their students with access to knowledge' (p.8).

This links with the discussion earlier in this chapter on 'powerful knowledge' which is concerned with introducing new ways of thinking that will empower children to think about alternative futures.

To help provide an overarching sense of the different curriculum-planning models, Kelly (1999 cited in Priestley, 2016) offers three models and explains that each model is cohesively linked with an underlying purpose and particular conception of knowledge, as well as a preferred pedagogical approach (Table 1.2).

Table 1.2   Curriculum planning models (Kelly, 1999 cited in Priestley, 2016)

Curriculum-planning model	Description
Curriculum as content and education as transmission	The starting point for this model is the content to be taught, often neglecting questions of purpose, and frequently conflating knowledge (an end of education) with subjects (one of various means available for accessing knowledge).
Curriculum as product and education as instrumental	In this approach, education is defined as assessable statements, such as learning outcomes, often specified in great detail across multiple linear levels. This approach has been associated with bureaucracy, over-assessment and instrumental 'tick-box' approaches to curriculum development (eg, Priestley and Minty, 2013).
Curriculum as process and education as development	In this approach, planning will start with consideration of purposes and values, and content and methods are selected to be fit for purpose. Process approaches can be complex and demanding on schools and teachers.

A curriculum can become technicist in its approach, which can result in learning becoming a disjointed 'tick-box' process, leading teachers to become too focused on checking that children have acquired competency (Priestley and Biesta, 2013) or the right type of knowledge (Hirsch, 1988; Young, 2014). Biesta and Priestley do argue that an appropriate task for curricula is to help emancipate students from the existing world to be able to foster a sense of critical democratic agency.

LEARNING

It is important to recognise that learning is not exclusively gained in the classroom environment but, like the discussions earlier regarding knowledge, what is counted as 'learning' will differ and depend on your point of view. Pritchard (2018) provides a useful table to portray the range of definitions concerning the process of learning (Table 1.3):

Table 1.3   Definitions of learning (Pritchard, 2018 p.1)

A change of behaviour as a result of experience of practice.
The acquisition of knowledge.
Knowledge gained through study.
To gain knowledge of, or skill in, something through study, teaching, instruction or experience.
The process of gaining knowledge. A process by which behaviour is changed, shaped or controlled.
The individual process of constructing understanding based on experience from a wide range of sources.

Unsurprisingly, there is a repetition of one specific key term: knowledge. There is also a recognition in a few of these definitions, that learning also occurs through experiences and how our behaviours or understanding are changed or reshaped by this (new) knowledge or experience. Learning plays a crucial role in understanding the concept of progress because it provides the path and the process with which we recognise children's progress.

Within school environments, learning can sometimes be interpreted as both process and, contra-dictorily, as a product. You may come across examples of this in your school setting where the term 'learning' has been used as an alternative to 'work', for example, teachers or support staff using expressions such as 'Talk to me about your learning'. Or in staff meetings, the term 'learning' almost being used as a synonym for 'productivity', for instance, 'How can we improve learning?'. Biesta (2015) would arguably attribute this to the increased 'learnification' of education and educational discourse. 'Learnification', Biesta explains, includes the rise of a 'new language of learning' within education. This new language includes referring to pupils, children and adults as 'learners' and the redefining of teaching as 'facilitating learning', 'learning opportunities' or 'learning experiences'. The expansive use of the term 'learning' within education, in particular, steps to conceptualise it as a 'product' rather than as a process, is arguably motivated by the need to capture and quantify this elusive concept for assessment and comparison purposes.

Pritchard (2018) argues that there has been a substantial reduction in time and opportunity to learning about 'learning', and the different theoretical standpoints on this process, within initial teacher education courses in the United Kingdom. This has arguably been in response to the emphasis by the government for beginning teachers to focus on 'what works' from those classrooms and schools that have been identified as 'successful'. During the time of Pritchard's writing, 2018, there may have been less emphasis, or perhaps less time available, on initial teacher training courses to ensure teachers knew about and understood the mechanics of the learning process. There is certainly, as Pritchard comments, some recognition in the Teachers' Standards which states, teachers must 'demonstrate knowledge and understanding of how pupils learn and how this impacts on teaching' (DfE, 2011). And that teachers are required to have a 'secure understanding of how a range of factors can inhibit pupils' ability to learn' (DfE, 2011). Perhaps part of the reason for the reduction of time being spent on learning theories is that they do not give teachers instantaneous ready-made tools to use in teaching (Brante et al., 2015 cited in Pritchard, 2018), which tends to be the preferred outcome in following a 'what works' approach. Despite this, Brante et al. do emphasis the critical value of classroom practice that is underpinned by a sound knowledge and understanding of current, and other relevant, theories related to learning.

ASSESSMENT

From nursery to university, children are constantly assessed (Wood, 2011), and with the adoption of the reception baseline, as we will see later in Chapters 2 and 3, this process seeks to start measuring pupil progress from the age of 4 (Richmond and Reagan, 2021). When considering the purpose and selection of specific assessment methods, McIntosh (DfE, 2015c p.18) explains that the following elements should be considered:

- Why pupils are being assessed.

- The things which the assessment is intended to measure.

- What the assessment is intended to achieve.

- How the assessment information will be used.

Wood (2011) argues that assessment could be interpreted more broadly to include even non-verbal cues from teachers, such as certain looks and gestures, which could also be recognised as forms of 'assessment'. The choice over which forms of assessment to use, or value, is dependent on how we interpret the nature and purpose of education. Additionally, how these are interpreted will be influenced by certain major players such as the government. As McIntosh (DfE, 2015c) explains, different forms of assessment can, and will, be used for different purposes by different interested parties and stakeholders, including pupils, parents, staff, school governors, the government, and of course Ofsted. For instance, national statutory assessments such as the standardised assessment tasks (SATs) are used by a range of individuals and organisations. For certain individuals and organisations, 'SATs are an invaluable tool for measuring the attainment and progress of both pupils and schools in an objective and consistent manner across England's 16,800 state-funded primary schools' (Richmond and Regan, 2021 p.1).

There are concerns that SATs can be a stressful, burdensome and potentially an unnecessary way to monitor pupils and schools, so they need to be reformed or scrapped completely (Richmond and Regan, 2021 p.1). Recently, research has shown that many teachers, researchers, educators and parents have been concerned about statutory assessment processes in England (Wyse et al., 2022). These concerns are motivated by the negative impact these assessments can have in presenting children as failures and be interpreted as a measurement of their future potential (Wood, 2011). For instance, a survey conducted by the National Education Union in 2018 found that 89 per cent of the 1,254 teacher respondents agreed that SATs had negatively affected pupils' wellbeing, and 86 per cent thought the SATs narrowed the curriculum (cited in Wyse et al., 2022). Furthermore, these types of assessments can reduce learning to the memorisation and regurgitation of facts and information, which particularly focus on propositional knowledge (Claxton, 2021).

This has plausibly contributed to schools feeling they needed to 'teach to the test' or narrow the curriculum (Richmond and Regan, 2021 p.70) to ensure children knew what they needed to know for the test. Evidence of this can be seen in Bradbury et al.'s (2021, cited in Wyse et al., 2022) study which reported that preparation for high-stakes assessments had altered both classroom and pedagogical practices, which included a narrowing of the curriculum. Claxton (2021) argues that these changes in pedagogical practices can rely on more knowledge transmission-based approaches, where teachers tell children important things; this is repeated to ensure children become proficient in memorising and demonstrating this knowledge in examination-like conditions. Concerns have been shared regarding the disruption caused by the COVID-19 pandemic widening gap, but the high stakes nature and stressful impact of statutory assessments have potentially compounded/exacerbated this issue. This was identified in Bradbury et al.'s (2021 cited in Wyse et al., 2022) study where participants discussed the increased use of interventions for certain prioritised pupils, who were recognised as 'borderline' in relation to national benchmarks, to enable them to 'catch up', similar to the practice, described by Gillborn and Youdell (1999 cited in Wyse et al., 2022) as *educational triage*, where specific groups of students are prioritised over others because they stand a better chance of demonstrating significant results, and consequently progress, in SATs tests.

Assessments play an essential role in the education system which has led to what Richardson (2022 cited in Wyse et al., 2022) has described as *assessment dysmorphia*, where the purpose of assessments has become distorted, resulting in a reduction of pupils' achievement in education, as assessments use a very narrow criteria to determine pupils' success. It is important to recognise that even though the situation is the way it is now, it does not necessarily have to continue to be that way. For instance, the British Educational Research Association expert panel released a report called *High Standards, not high stakes* (Moss et al., 2021) that presented an alternative assessment system to the present SATs system we have at present. The report recommended the removal of all annual tests which would be replaced with a longitudinal sample of pupils. This approach would arguably allow for contextual variables such as the location and size of the school, the makeup of the catchment area and diversity of the student population in the area. Another two key recommendations, as part of the overhaul of the present system, would be the formation of new organisation to act independently of the government and a different inspection process. Other researchers such as Nuthall (2001) provide an alternatives perspective on knowledge, arguing that it is more of a continuous landscape, rather than a set of discrete countable objects, which consequently means knowledge cannot be accurately understood, or be quantitatively represented as a number. He argues that the scores that pupils receive on tests are 'primarily the result of the students' motivations and cultural background, and only secondarily about what the student knows or can do'.

CRITIQUING REDUCTIVE VIEWS OF PROGRESS

If we understand progress to be 'learning' that is recognised, measured and accounted for, then it becomes very important to understand how (and why) this happens, and the underlying assumptions behind what seems to be a reductive perception towards progress. Conceptualising 'progress' as knowing more and remembering more (Ofsted, 2019a) conveys a particular view regarding 'progress' and 'learning' and how the process of learning is captured (eg, the assessment of this learning to help identify progress). The complex origins behind these 'reductive' interpretations towards progress will be explored in further detail in the Final thoughts and reflections section. It is important though to briefly question this motivation to quantify progress, to an also numerical level, and the potential impact it has in reducing our perception of learning as something only to be known and remembered.

An example of this influence can be seen in children's progress in reading. In the 2021 Progress in International Reading Literacy Study (PIRLS), England moved up to fourth place (from joint eighth place in 2016). In response to this outcome, former Minister of State for Schools Nick Gibb attributed this result to consistent commitment in England to teaching systematic synthetic phonics (SSP) in schools (Martin, 2023). Currently in England, direct SSP instruction is started with children aged 4–5 (Reception) as stipulated in the Early Years Foundation Stage curriculum. This direct instruction is continued with children aged 5–6 (Year 1) through SSP lessons over two years, as specified in the National Curriculum and the reading framework (Wyse, 2023a). This process intensifies and culminates with Year 1 children completing the phonics screening check. The purpose behind this test is to 'confirm that all children have learnt phonic decoding to an age-appropriate standard' (STAb, 2017 p.4). It was believed that using the phonics screening check would increase the number of children who could read competently by the time they reached the end of Key Stages 1 and 2 (STAb, 2017).

One of the criticisms of the check is that it narrowly focuses on decoding, so children do well in the phonics screening check, but this does nothing to encourage a love of reading. Additionally, concerns were voiced that assessing just decoding skills could led to schools just exclusively focussing on phonics training as the only way to learn to read. Arguably, the result of this approach was recognised in the 2021 PIRLS study which asked children directly about how much they liked reading and found that England was 42nd out of 57 countries (Wyse, 2023b). So, despite moving to fourth place for progress in reading, Wyse identifies that the 2021 PIRLS data state that 24 per cent of England's pupils said that they did not like reading; 48 per cent said they somewhat like reading; and only 29 per cent said they very much like reading.

It is possible to see how several concerns have been raised regarding the exclusive use of explicit phonics instruction as the only way to learn to read and the impact this is having on children's enjoyment of reading, which is recognised and encouraged in the national curriculum. Gee (2004) argues that instructed processes (such as SSP) involve practising skills divorced from the context of reading (eg, books that interest readers) and neglect the other important reading skills used by more adept readers. Gee identifies that children become successful readers because learning is a cultural process, rather than purely an instructed one; this includes children being exposed to books, reading with others and developing a love of reading. Instructed processes of teaching, and tests such as the phonics screening check, perceive progress in reading through a technicist lens, causing teachers to become more focused on checking that children have acquired competency (Biesta and Priestley, 2013) or that the right type of knowledge has been learnt (Hirsch, 1988; Young, 2014). It leads to a reductionist interpretation of reading, which primarily perceives decoding and reading as synonymous with one another.

Part of this interpretation can be attributed to the focus and pressure of the phonics screening check, and its reductive nature to what qualifies as learning. Evidence of this was captured by Wyse and Bradbury (2022) in their survey of 2,200 teachers, 936 of whom were negative about the compulsory screening check and commented that they felt pressured to teach to the test. This leads us back to the issue of *assessment dysmorphia* (Richardson, 2022 cited in Wyse et al., 2022) where assessments such as these result in a reduction of pupil achievement in education, as assessments use a very narrow criteria to determine pupils' success. Gee states that those who advocate that children are poor readers because they have received poor skills instruction early on in school tend to perceive reading in a reductive way. This leads to early and overt phonics instruction being considered the solution to the issue of poor reading. This is openly stated in the phonics screening check guidance which states that process should 'identify children who have not learned to decode using phonics by the end of Year 1. These children will then receive additional support to ensure they can improve their decoding skills' (STA, 2017b p.5). So, children who are assessed with reading difficulties are given even more intensive SSP instruction (Wyse, 2023a). Rather than bringing children up to the same standard as those who are considered confident readers, Gee argues that more intensive phonics instruction for those readers who struggle can put them at a greater disadvantage compared to their more privileged peers because they are not receiving a balanced reading experience that include cultural process of learning.

We have already discussed that learning occurs through various experiences and that our behaviours, or our understanding, are changed or reshaped by this (new) knowledge or experience. Our interpretation of learning, and what counts as learning, does play a significant role in how we understand the concept of progress as it provides the path and the insight into what we recognise as 'progress'. We need to be mindful as teachers that reductive interpretations do not hold sway over us. Indeed, Wyse (2023a) suggests that a clear emphasis on phonics is necessary, but he does caution that this should not be taught exclusively through separate synthetic phonics lessons. He instead suggests there needs to be a more balanced approach which incorporates other important aspects in the teaching of reading, such as comprehension, motivation for reading and engagement with real books rather than just an exclusive diet of decodable books. This balanced approach considers other interpretations of learning, and aspects that perhaps cannot be quantified so easily and succinctly, such as reading enjoyment, but nonetheless play a significant role in children's learning, and their motivation to learn.

REFLECTIVE QUESTIONS

- What is currently your understanding of progress in the classroom?
- What do you consider to be 'knowledge'?
- Have you seen reductive views of progress in the classroom?
- How has reading this chapter challenged your perspective towards 'progress'?

2

NATIONAL CONTEXT 1988–2014

KEY WORDS: AGE-RELATED EXPECTATIONS; ASSESSMENT; BENCHMARKS; FORMATIVE; LEVELS; MASTERY; NATIONAL CURRICULUM; STANDARD; STATUTORY; SUMMATIVE

THE HISTORY OF CURRICULUM AND STATUTORY MEASURES OF ATTAINMENT AND PROGRESS

This chapter takes you through the history of approaches to measuring progress in primary schools and is important in helping you to understand the decisions that might be made in your school and support you in the decisions that you will make in your classroom day to day. Linking to the themes developed in the previous section, we can see that any approach to measuring progress has, implicit within it, assumptions around what is knowledge, what curricula should encompass and how children's attainment, and progress through those curricula, might be set and measured.

THE INTRODUCTION OF THE NATIONAL CURRICULUM AND TRACKING PROGRESS THROUGH LEVELS

Following the introduction of a national curriculum (HMSO, 1988) and the use of end of key stage test data in making judgements about primary schools by the Ofsted inspectorate (HMSO, 1992), schools became very focussed on the production and analysis of numerical data. By the end of the 1990s, local authorities (LAs) had become increasingly involved, challenging schools to set attainment and progress targets for English (reading and writing), mathematics and science based on calculations and comparisons for children through from the Early Years to KS1 and onwards to KS2 and 3 (Hedger and Jesson, 1999), although KS3 tests were later abandoned (HMSO, 2009).

With test and teacher assessment outcomes presented in the form of national curriculum 'expected levels' from 1 to 8, charts and graphs showing progress from one key stage to another were used extensively to show whether schools were enabling children in similar groups (prior attainment, school characteristics) to make more progress than the 'expected progress' of two national curriculum levels between key stages. Subdividing each level into three (1c, 1b, 1a, etc.) enabled the levels to be converted into 'point scores' ranging in primary schools from 3 for a child deemed 'Working Towards level 1' (or 'W') to 41 for 64 (Table 2.1). The two-level progress could then be made more granular and progress from Key Stage 1 to 2 could be mapped in more detail on to a line graph. To generate data summarising a whole school performance, an average point score was calculated from the results of the statutory English and mathematics tests combined. This enabled schools to be compared through the percentage above or below the national average in terms of attainment and progress.

Table 2.1 *Expected progress through national curriculum levels*

Level (point score)	Yr1	Yr2	Yr3	Yr4	Yr5	Yr6
6 (37–41)						
5a (35)						
5b (33)						
5c (31)						
4a (29)						
4b (27)						
4c (25)						
3a (23)						
3b (21)						
3c (19)						
2a (17)						
2b (15)						
2c (13)						
1a (11)						
1b (9)						
1c (7)						
W (3)						

The aim for individual schools was to match, or better, the national figures, not just for attainment reaching the desired level but also for making 'expected' or 'more than expected' progress between key stages. Central government provided a range of comparative data and tools to enable schools, LAs and Ofsted inspectors to make these comparisons between individual and groups of schools in the local area or nationally. Schools were encouraged to target as many children as possible not just to reach the 'expected level' (level 4b by the end of Key Stage 2) but also to exceed this (4a, or preferably level 5, or even 6) and to make not just 'expected progress' between key stages (2 levels, or 6 points) but also 'more than expected progress' (7 points or more).

This approach had an impact on how progress was measured in other year groups and target setting based on how many points progress children should be making each year in order to guarantee 'more than expected progress' over the key stage. Schools used their management systems such as SIMs, bought-in packages or their own spreadsheets to manage, analyse and present the data produced by in-school assessment processes. The government provided additional materials to support schools in making national curriculum level judgements about individual pupil performance, not only through optional tests but also through assessment support resources, including descriptive rubrics such as the Assessing Pupil Progress (APP) materials and exemplars demonstrating national curriculum attainment for all levels. LAs also provided guidance and target setting challenges. Foundation subjects, of course, were not part of the national picture; however, with such clear frameworks for core subjects, if schools tracked children's progress in these subjects in any sort of detail, or indeed at all, similar systems were often applied.

A NEW GOVERNMENT, A NEW CURRICULUM

When a new coalition (Conservatives and Liberal Democrats) formed a government following elections in March 2010, a review (DfE, 2011a) of the curriculum took place and a new curriculum for Key Stages 1–3 planned. Following a draft for consultation in February (DfE, 2013a), it was finalised in October, and introduced from 2014 (DfE, 2013b).

The published new national curriculum removed levels altogether. It outlined what was to be taught to children, laying out the content to be covered at particular ages, removing the expectation that children should make accelerated progress. The curriculum itself gave no guidance on assessment or what exactly children should achieve in relation to content laid out more discretely in year group terms for core subjects (English, mathematics and science). Perhaps sometimes overlooked, in the introduction, it emphasises that the year group/content relationship is not statutory, simply a suggestion of how the content could be covered over time:

> The key stage 2 programmes of study for English, mathematics and science are presented in this document as 'lower' (years 3 and 4) and 'upper' (years 5 and 6). This distinction is made as guidance for teachers and is not reflected in legislation. The legal requirement is to cover the content of the programmes of study for years 3 to 6 by the end of key stage 2.
>
> (DfE, 2014c)

It is stated even more explicitly in each of the subject sections for English (p.17), mathematics (p.109) and science (p.169):

> The programmes of study for [English] [mathematics] [science] are set out year-by-year for key stages 1 and 2. Schools are, however, only required to teach the relevant programme of study by the end of the key stage. Within each key stage, schools therefore have the flexibility to introduce content earlier or later than set out in the programme of study. In addition, schools can introduce key stage content during an earlier key stage, if appropriate.
>
> (DfE, 2013b)

Expected outcomes, in the broadest terms, were only mentioned in relation to the whole of the key stage content (following each subject's purpose and aims, before the content, and under the heading 'Attainment Targets'):

> By the end of each key stage, pupils are expected to know, apply, and understand the matters, skills and processes specified in the relevant programme of study.
>
> (DfE, 2013b)

ASSESSMENT WITHOUT LEVELS AND IMPLICATIONS FOR MEASURING PROGRESS: DAY TO DAY, OVER TIME, STATUTORY

Assessment presented a significant change for schools, perhaps even greater than the curriculum itself. For almost all teachers working in schools at this time of change, measuring attainment and progress had always been linked closely to the curriculum through extensive government guidance. Only the end of key stage assessment had been statutory; however, optional materials provided by government combined with pressure channelled through LAs and Ofsted, had structured approaches to assessing the attainment children in all year groups. The implications for school progress tracking meant that schools across the country were using the same language, the same materials and similar bought in packages. A child could move from Manchester to Brighton to Penzance, and the schools would all be applying similar and recognisable assessment standards and measuring systems across all year groups. Ofsted inspectors would recognise school tracking systems and readily understand what schools were trying to achieve through their target setting from year to year, and consequently, across the school.

The period following the publication of the curriculum and guidance around assessment, including the assessment and tracking of progress, was unsettled, and demonstrates the challenge of agreeing new ways of thinking about attainment and progress, especially in the context of standardisation. The idea of moving quickly through content was well established and embedded in tracking systems and target setting.

SETTING THE BENCHMARKS

Although no specific guidance was given at the time the new curriculum was launched, Tim Oates (Cambridge Assessment, online n.d.), the chair of the curriculum expert panel, had made some clear points with regard to assessment with and without levels. He had emphasised a slenderer curriculum, with a focus on developing depth. He asserted: 'Assessment should focus on whether children have understood these key concepts rather than achieved a particular level'. This would be a fundamental change, given the shared approach through levels, agreed national standards in core subjects for all year groups and expected rates of progress which had been easily represented graphically.

At this stage, there was no clarity as to what exactly constituted the 'expected standard' for children in each year group, or how either attainment or progress were to be measured. Even statutory assessment at the end of the key stages was to lag behind the introduction of the curriculum since children in Year 2 and 6 had not been taught its content as they moved through the key stage and these new assessments were not in place until the summer of 2016.

The government had outlined descriptors for the end of key stages (DfE, 2014a). Although the number of levels for subjects were inconsistent, the five proposed levels for KS2 writing were:

- Mastery standard

- Above national standard

- National standard

- Working towards national standard

- Below national standard.

These descriptors also came at a time when the idea of 'mastery', although not new, was becoming popular, particularly in relation to mathematics. The Cambridge Review Trust respondents (2014 p.14) write:

Mastery is also a problematic term. Surely if children have met the national standard that implies that they are competent for their age in that area.

In this case, 'mastery' is seen as synonymous with 'competent'; certainly, others seem to ascribe something similar. The Education Endowment Foundation attempts a definition at a 'mastery learning' method which provides time for all pupils to become 'competent or proficient'.

Traditional teaching keeps time spent on a topic constant and allows pupils' 'mastery' of curriculum content to vary. Mastery learning keeps learning outcomes constant but varies the time needed for pupils to become proficient or competent at these objectives.

This interpretation, however, seemed to be at odds with the two levels of achievement above the national standard for KS2 writing listed in the descriptor proposals which seem to suggest that mastery is something far and beyond expectations – not just above, but something even more.

Since these first iterations of the frameworks, there have been a number of changes, but the very first versions did remove the 'mastery' that had been found contentious within the drafts and seemed to respond to the points in the reports which had been received positively. The descriptors were presented as a list of 'I can' statements, all of which must be met unlike the APP materials, a 'best-fit' approach was not intended. The number of bands (or levels) within each curriculum area was still inconsistent: for Key Stage 1, there were to be three for reading, writing and mathematics, but just one for science, and for Key Stage 2, there were three for writing, but just one for reading, mathematics and science. However, where there were three bands or levels they were, and still are (for example, DFE, 2018a,b), presented as:

- Working towards the expected standard

- Working within the expected standard

- Working at greater depth within the expected standard

However, confusion about the term 'mastery', and the introduction of this new term 'greater depth' for writing, had an impact on the systems schools set up to measure attainment and progress after 2014. Although there is some guidance within the documents of when particular content could be taught, the curriculum is presented statutorily as content to be covered over a whole key stage, to be tested at the end; what then does mastery, the expected standard or greater depth look like for any curriculum content in Year 3, in Year 5? How do we track progress from one year to another?

The government response to the consultation of the Department of Education (DfE) had again emphasised the separation between statutory and in-school assessment systems (DfE, 2015a):

The removal of levels was based on the principle that schools are best placed to develop their own high-quality formative assessment systems, which are diagnostic, and which are not necessarily nationally referenced. The intention of the performance descriptors is to provide summative assessment at the end of Key Stages 1 and 2 only. They are not intended to inform ongoing assessment...

and it highlighted concerns that had been raised that 'performance descriptors could be applied to formative assessment in a way that is not intended'.

This separation between the end of key stages and the years in between was new. In school assessment processes, formative assessment up until now had been based on a clear trajectory from Year 1 right through to Year 6, at least in core subjects.

BREAKING THE LINK: STATUTORY, IN SCHOOL SUMMATIVE AND IN SCHOOL FORMATIVE ASSESSMENT

Alongside the development of the new curriculum, a consultation on assessment and accountability had been set up in July 2013, with responses sought by October (DfE, 2013e) and a response in 2014 (DfE, 2014b). In part to address concerns, but also to explore best practice, it announced the proposed launch of a Commission for Assessment Without Levels (CAWL), led by John McIntosh, referred to previously (DfE, 2015b). The commission was subsequently set up, with its members announced in July 2015 and a report (DfE, 2015c) and the government's response published in September (DfE, 2015d) along with final performance descriptors (DfE, 2015e,f) now called 'assessment frameworks' to underpin teacher assessment at the end of key stages.

The consultation made two clear points relative to pupil progress:

1. Formative assessment was to be separated from summative assessment.

2. Schools would be able to develop their own in-school systems of tracking progress looking forward to the end of the key stage.

> There will be a clear separation between ongoing, formative assessment (wholly owned by schools) and the statutory summative assessment which the government will prescribe to provide robust external accountability and national benchmarking. [...] Ofsted will expect to see evidence of pupils' progress, with inspections informed by the school's chosen pupil tracking data.

> The assessment framework must be built into the school curriculum, so that schools can check what pupils have learnt and whether they are on track to meet expectations at the end of the key stage.

(2013e pp.5, 8)

The final CAWL report (DfE, 2015c) summarised some of the issues, some already raised in earlier documents from the DfE and the curriculum panel, resulting from the use of national curriculum levels. It emphasises most strongly the separation between statutory and in-school assessment and guards against the using of systems, including commercial packages, modelled on statutory assessment. Below are some extracts from the document. Spend some time reflecting on these, in relation to the systems in your school. You may find it useful to jot down some notes to remind you when you come to respond to the reflective questions in Chapter 4.

> Levels were used to measure both end of phase achievement and lesson-by-lesson formative progress, but they had not been designed to fulfil the latter purpose, with the result that formative assessment was often distorted.

> Assessment without levels gives schools the opportunity to develop their own approaches to assessment that focus on teaching and learning and are tailored to the curriculum followed by the school.

formative assessments do not have to be measured using the same scale that is used for summative assessments. For this reason, the Commission urges schools to **guard against designing or purchasing assessment systems modelled on statutory arrangements for teacher assessment,** *regardless of how these may change over time.*

Removing levels encourages schools to develop approaches to in-school assessment which are better tied to curriculum content, and which **do not restrict teaching solely to the specific content in the National curriculum but** encourage the wider exploration of subjects which results in higher attainment and greater enjoyment.

In-school summative assessment should not be driven by nationally collected forms of statutory summative assessment. What works best for national accountability purposes does not necessarily work best for supporting teaching and learning or for monitoring pupil progress.

(2015d pp.14–24. Our bold)

It also develops Tim Oates' emphasis on focussing on facilitating depth in learning, seeking to clarify the concept of 'mastery', its use becoming more widespread. He describes it as the aim for all children to achieve in discrete steps before they move on to new content. Built into this understanding of the term is that 'the assumption that all pupils will achieve this level of mastery if they are appropriately supported. Some may take longer and need more help, but all will get there in the end' (Cambridge Assessment, online n.d.).

Thus, it is not a higher level of attainment for some children, but an aspiration for all, and an expectation that teachers will find ways to facilitate this. One could argue, this is the elusive 'expected standard'.

The government's response consolidated this and again cautions schools in their choice of external systems:

The Commission's definition of mastery in assessment is particularly helpful and reflects an underpinning principle of the new curriculum that pupils should achieve a secure and deep understanding of the whole curriculum content before being moved on to new content. It is important that schools, and those who support schools, have a clear and singular definition of mastery.

We support the Commission's views that schools should properly consider the merits of external assessment systems and ensure value for money before investing in any products.

(DfE, 2015d pp.4–5)

THE STUBBORNNESS OF THE LINK

Following the changes to the curriculum and its assessment, the parliament's education select committee set up an enquiry into primary assessment in September 2016 and reported the following April (HOC, 2017a). The government responded in October (HOC, 2017b).

The report forwarded a blunt judgement:

National curriculum levels were removed without enough support in place for schools to implement their own assessment systems successfully. Many schools have now adopted ineffective assessment systems.

(HOC, 2017a para 47)

The government responded by agreeing that national curriculum levels had come to dominate all assessment practice despite the original intention being for them to be specifically for end of key stage assessment. It did not acknowledge that in this respect, little may have changed. The response offers the CAWL report as the government approach to mitigating the danger of this being repeated now that levels had gone and suggests this is the guidance that schools can use 'as they develop their own assessment systems':

> We recognise that the removal of levels was a significant change for schools. Levels were only ever intended to be used for end-of-key stage statutory assessment, but over time they came to dominate all assessment and teaching practice. This had a damaging impact on teaching and failed to give parents an accurate understanding of how their children achieved.

The National Foundation for Educational Research (NFER) reported the same issues:

> The influence of statutory national is still clearly apparent in schools' non-statutory assessment and continues to be the main driver for formative and summative assessment.

(NFER, 2018 p.10)

The National Association of Head Teachers' Assessment Review Group made the same point:

> It is all too easy for statutory assessment to become entangled with in-school assessment [...] in-school assessments inevitably take on the form of statutory assessments, in order to produce compatible data, however inappropriate this form may be to support teaching and learning.

(NAHT, 2017 p.7)

BACK TO BENCHMARKING: THE DEVELOPMENT OF AGE-RELATED EXPECTATIONS

Despite the emphasis from so many quarters on the separation of statutory assessment from in-school assessment, and the clarity within the national curriculum itself that the statutory requirement was only that the content be covered by the end of the key stage, the application of 'age-related expectations' (AREs) now seems ubiquitous for every year group. Despite its widespread use, finding the origin of the term has proved difficult. It does not exist in the national curriculum document, in the CAWL report or the government response, in the STA statutory assessment arrangements (STA, 2023d) or in the end of key stage assessment frameworks (STA, 2017a and updates), yet within purchased or school-designed tracking systems, on school websites, from bodies and from organisations such as NFER (2016 and website), The School Run (ND) subject hubs and LAs, it is presented as a definitive term, not just for the end of the key stage but also for every discrete year group. The examples that can be found online, although reflecting areas of the national curriculum for the relevant year group, are inconsistent. A presentation given at Bath Spa University (Pembroke, 2016) provides a clear overview of how AREs, or year group objectives, are being used to reproduce a system not unlike national curriculum levels.

The NFER itself, besides authoring the 2018 report, provides optional year group tests in reading and mathematics for school use, which apply the term to these test outcomes. Writing about the concept on its website, there is an acknowledgement that it is not based on government guidance. It does not acknowledge the non-statutory link between content and year group in the national curriculum documents. As they say:

> *As the government does not publish expected standards for other year groups across key stage 1 and 2*, NFER has developed its own age-related expectations for its summer reading and mathematics tests. These are designed to help teachers identify whether pupils in Years 1–5 have achieved the standard on the national curriculum, which is appropriate for their year group, by the time they have taken the test.
>
> NFER's age-related expectations have been developed by undertaking a rigorous standard setting process with assessment experts and a diverse group of experienced teachers in order to agree the thresholds. Age-related expectations have been established for NFER's summer tests only because it is at this point that pupils can be expected to have been taught the national curriculum content for that year group.
>
> (NFER, website)

While the schools involved in the 2018 NFER research reported an increased focus on formative assessment, and improved feedback and communication with students, it did not explore the assumptions, knowledge, understanding and purpose which formed the basis of schools' decision-making. In particular, there was no reference to how these new ways of assessing and tracking progress were understood to tackle the perceived issues around the use of levels, including those highlighted by the report from the expert panel that reviewed the national curriculum between 2010 and 2011 (DfE, 2011a) and remarks on assessment by its chair, Tim Oates (Cambridge Assessment, online n.d.), the CAWL's report (2015c) and the government response (2015d). Thus, we might raise questions on three interrelated themes:

- How do schools perceive the underlying intentions of the new curriculum?

- How does in-school formative assessment relate to those intentions?

- On what basis have decisions been made around the choice of in-school assessment processes and tracking systems?

In 2023, things have changed and are set to change further. Two particular developments have had, or will have, an impact. Firstly, the changes to the Ofsted framework and focus from September 2019 (Ofsted, 2019a and updates). This framework emphasised that inspectors are looking at how in-school data are designed and used, and not for any specific approach. An Ofsted blog (2018) and video (Ofsted, 2019b) reminded us of not just the importance but also the potential negative impact of over reliance on performance tables and headline measures. The blog emphasises that 'expected progress' was removed as an accountability measure in 2015 and that by progress they mean 'pupils knowing more and remembering more'. Ofsted would not be looking at in-school data, but would spend time observing and discussing with pupils and staff to gather evidence of the quality of education, built on a strong and 'good curriculum, well taught'. Subsequent updates to the framework have not strayed from this position.

Secondly, statutory measures of progress have changed. Key Stage 2 Standard Assessment Tests have been discontinued, and, with the introduction of the baseline assessment (DfE, 2019a, 2023b), progress between reception and Key Stage 2 will form the basis of government statistics for schools (DfE, 2019b, 2023e). Early Years practitioners have become familiar over many years with assessing outcomes for young children applying a very different system from that in Key Stages 1 and 2. This will no doubt continue for measuring progress through the reception year, working with the non-statutory development matters (DfE, 2023f) alongside the Early Years Foundation Stage (EYFS) curriculum framework (DfE, 2023c). The differences in both curriculum and assessment have sometimes led to reception outcomes being transformed into the sort of numerical data which can be tacked on to the beginning of spreadsheet-based tracking systems in order to monitor and manage progress from reception to Year 1 and then on to 2. The baseline assessment may be the most obvious answer to marrying up the two systems to demonstrate progress but assumes the numbers are measuring factors which are comparable. Although there may be some support for measuring progress through the whole of primary school, the difficulties about how this can be achieved means the proposal as planned, and its final implementation, has met with some opposition. The final agreed assessment is quite different from those familiar EYFS assessment methods of detailed daily observations and conversations, is completed within 20 minutes and returns a score out of 39.

It does mean, however, that schools remain ever conscious of the need to be aware of progress towards very specific, externally set and measured expected progress goals; these will be built into target setting and tracking systems. There are examples of attempts to separate the final expected outcome from in-school assessment (Third Space Learning, 2020), but perhaps while accountability for school leaders continues to depend on the outcome of statutory assessment progress measures between specified year groups, this remains an aspiration which is hard to meet in practical terms.

Thinking back to the work of the Assessment Reform Group (ARG, 2002) on the principles of formative assessment, we should be aware of the links formed between accountability and assessment which threaten the use of assessment as a teaching tool, which facilitates pupil progress, and the development of complex and time-consuming tracking systems, which quantify progress and reproduce the unhelpful approaches to assessment that the removal of levels was intended to tackle. The previous chief inspector, Amanda Spielman, recognised some of these issues and, additionally, emphasised the impact on teacher workload (Spielman, 2018). Assessment must be intended to support progress and ultimately to raise standards. The CAWL report and subsequent documents make it very clear: in-school processes are intended to be focussed on individual and class or cohort progress. The choice about what to assess and the systems they use is for schools to decide upon. Statutory assessment is a government accountability measure for schools against clear and limited criteria.

This, then, seems a key moment at which to reconsider the questions posed earlier, this time specifically from your own perspective.

REFLECTIVE QUESTIONS

- What do you understand as the intentions of the removal of national curriculum levels?
- What influences your decision-making around assessment and tracking of pupil progress; what sources of advice, support or resources are drawn upon?
- Does your practice in assessing and tracking pupil progress fulfil the stated intentions of the 2014 national curriculum, the CAWL report and the government's response at the time?
- What is your attitude to the systems in place (purpose, effectiveness, impact on pupil progress, workload and personal investment in the process and outcomes)?

PART 2
PROGRESS IN YOUR SCHOOL

LINKS TO THE CORE CONTENT FRAMEWORK
(CORE CONTENT AND EARLY CAREER FRAMEWORK)

Standard 1 – 'Set high expectations'

1.3. Teacher expectations can affect pupil outcomes; setting goals that challenge and stretch pupils *(from their starting point)* is essential.

Standard 2 – 'Promote good progress'

2.1. Learning involves a lasting change in pupils' capabilities or understanding.

2.2. Prior knowledge plays an important role in how pupils learn; committing some key facts to their long-term memory is likely to help pupils learn more complex ideas.

Standard 3 – 'Demonstrate good subject and curriculum knowledge'

3.1. A school's curriculum enables it to set out its vision for the knowledge, skills and values that its pupils will learn, encompassing the national curriculum within a coherent wider vision for successful learning.

3.3. Ensuring pupils master foundational concepts and knowledge before moving on is likely to build pupils' confidence and help them succeed.

3.5. Explicitly teaching pupils the knowledge and skills they need to succeed within particular subject areas is beneficial.

3.7. In all subject areas, pupils learn new ideas by linking those ideas to existing knowledge, organising this knowledge into increasingly complex mental models (or 'schemata'); carefully sequencing teaching to facilitate this process is important.

Standard 6 – 'Make accurate and productive use of assessment'

6.1. Effective assessment is critical to teaching because it provides teachers with information about pupils' understanding and needs.

6.3. Before using any assessment, teachers should be clear about the decision that it will be used to support and be able to justify its use.

6.7. Working with colleagues to identify efficient approaches to assessment is important; assessment can become onerous and have a disproportionate impact on workload.

3
THE CURRENT NATIONAL CONTEXT

KEY WORDS: ACCOUNTABILITY; ASSESSMENT; CURRICULUM; EXPECTATIONS; INSPECTION; PROGRESS MEASURES

The first part of this book raised some broad and important issues by asking you to consider more closely how progress is interpreted within education by briefly examining the concepts of knowledge, curriculum, learning and assessment. In discussing these, we come to understand that these concepts, rather than existing as clear, obvious and value free, are in fact highly influenced by reductionist type values and choices. The power of these values can be seen in what is recognised as 'knowledge' (and what is not), which influences what is included, and excluded, within curricula. Furthermore, we are introduced to the complex process of learning and how these values attempt to reduce and assess learning by capturing and quantifying it as product. We begin to understand the implications of this for children who may not neatly fit or thrive within an education system based on such reductionist perspectives and values.

It then went on to outline key changes in the national curriculum and assessment, particularly those that came about following the general election in March 2010. The new government changed the structure of the curriculum in significant ways and, consequently, the ways in which attainment and progress are measured. The intention of the removal of national curriculum levels was to move away from accelerating progress towards mastery and depth of taught material. However, systems and processes for benchmarking attainment and measuring progress which had become embedded in schools, in the absence of nationally provided frameworks, have proved difficult to shift. We could argue, at least for English and mathematics, that schools have simply applied old ways of thinking about progress to a new curriculum which was intended to change the way we thought about both attainment and progress, and that schools have failed to take up the opportunity offered to them to track progress in their own way, appropriate for their own contexts. Prior to 2014, schools knew what attainment at different ages and progress from Early Years to Year 6 was supposed to look like and how it could be measured and represented graphically. Now there is no such clarity. Schools are still held accountable for core outcomes at the end of Year 6, and there is clear guidance to be had regarding that for core subjects, but any framework for progress towards that point is schools for the making.

This chapter builds on this, now outlining the current context for schools and the staff who work in them. We will look at curriculum expectations for schools and accountability through inspection and outcomes for children, and at accountability for individual teachers. These are the frameworks, systems and processes within which schools work. They act as a basis for strategic planning for trusts, local authorities (LAs), school leaders at all levels and individual teachers. They generate criteria and rubrics for monitoring and moderating practice, and for evaluation and accountability. Crucially, although many of these are statutory, there is often scope for local interpretation and application; indeed, schools have been clearly encouraged to make their own choices when it comes to tracking progress. As you read through these, think back to what you have previously read, and keep in mind the reflective questions.

┌───┐

REFLECTIVE QUESTIONS

What do we understand by progress?

- As educators, what are our aims for the children we work with as they move from Early Years to Year 6 and beyond?

- What aspects of school achievement are important to target and track?

- What criteria will we use to capture attainment and track progress in those aspects? How will we generate and structure them?

- What shared, accessible and inclusive language will we use to describe what we are doing: with each other, and with children?

- Have we thought creatively about what we do, so as not to repeat the problems of the past?

- Do we recognise the implications of the choices we make, for every child, for those who work with them, for parents and carers and for communities and society as a whole?

└───┘

CURRICULUM

There are two key curriculum documents that apply to children in primary schools in England: the national curriculum for Key Stages 1 and 2 (DfE, 2013a), and a framework for the Early Years Foundation Stage (EYFS) (DfE 2023c), which applies to children from birth to 5. The first statutory school year, reception, is the last year of the EYFS. These curricula are statutory in all maintained schools. This does not include academies, but most academies will follow the national curriculum, and their pupils' attainment and progress in core subjects will be measured at the end of Key Stage 2 according to its content. Religious education is not a national curriculum subject, nor does it appear explicitly in the EYFS framework, but it is statutory for all children on the school roll though a locally agreed syllabus. Relationships education is supported by published guidance. Table 3.1 sets out the subjects which are included in these two documents and other statutory guidance.

Table 3.1 *Early Years Foundation Stage (EYFS) and national curriculum content*

	EYFS		Key Stage 1	Key Stage 2
National curriculum/EYFS				
Core subjects	Prime area	Specific area		
English	Communication and language	Literacy	Yes	Yes
Mathematics		Mathematics	Yes	Yes
Science		Understanding the world	Yes	Yes

Table 3.1 (Continued)

		EYFS	Key Stage 1	Key Stage 2
Foundation subjects				
Art and design		Expressive arts and design	Yes	Yes
Citizenship	Personal, social and emotional development		Not statutory	Not statutory
Computing	No		Yes	Yes
Design and technology		Expressive arts and design	Yes	Yes
Languages	No		Yes	Yes
Geography	Understanding the world		Yes	Yes
History	Understanding the world		Yes	Yes
Music			Yes	Yes
Physical education	Physical development		Yes	Yes
Personal, social, health and economic	Personal, social and emotional development		Content not specified	Content not specified
Other statutory subjects				
Religious education	In line with an agreed syllabus		Yes	Yes
Sex and relationship education	personal, social and emotional development		Relationships education	Relationships education

This is a national curriculum. Conceived in 1988 (HMSO, 1988) as an entitlement for all children, the original curriculum, and its following iterations, was always intended as a minimum entitlement, not a complete curriculum.

In the buildup to the present curriculum, the expert panel reported to the DfE (2011a) and made clear:

> It is important to distinguish between the National Curriculum and the wider school curriculum (the whole curriculum as experienced by pupils in each school). There are a number of components of a broad and balanced school curriculum that should be developed on the basis of local or school-level decision making, rather than prescribed national Programmes of Study. To facilitate this, the National Curriculum should not absorb the overwhelming majority of teaching time in schools.

And also:

> We recommend that the National Curriculum review should be framed by awareness of fundamental educational processes so that the necessary attention to curricular detail does not take place without

regard to its consequences for the curriculum as a whole. In particular, this should include consideration of the basic interaction between subject knowledge and individual development.

DfE (2011a pp.6–7)

The present curriculum aims to:

- embody rigour and high standards and create coherence in what is taught in schools.

- ensure that all children are taught the essential knowledge in the key subject disciplines.

- go beyond that core, to allow teachers greater freedom to use their professionalism and expertise to help all children realise their potential.

DfE (2013d)

When considering progress, it is easy to think of its content not merely as a core around which other curriculum content might develop but as our sole focus. We come later to thinking about the significant impact the national curriculum, and the portions of it that are assessed statutorily, has on the ways in which schools characterise progress.

The purpose of any curriculum is to set out what is to be taught, not about how it might be assessed, or benchmarks for tracking progress through the content. As we will discuss in the next section, apart from very focussed assessments for phonics decoding in Year 1 (STA, 2023a) and multiplication tables in Year 4 (STA, 2022), outcomes are now only nationally tested at the end of Key Stage 2, with a new baseline at the start of school from which to measure progress: it is at these points that we have national standards against which children are assessed, and these standards only cover core subjects. Year 2 assessments, previously statutory, are now optional but will continue to be available for schools to use and will be updated (STA, 2023b). This means that school have nationally shared criteria available for core subjects at the end of the key stage, but not for benchmarking along the way. The way the content is set out may give guidance as to what elements of the curriculum could be taught at what age, but not what standards of attainment might look like at that point. And as made clear earlier, the distinctive content for lower and upper KS2 in core subjects is not statutory:

The key stage 2 programmes of study for English, mathematics and science are presented in this document as 'lower' (years 3 and 4) and 'upper' (years 5 and 6). This distinction is made as guidance for teachers and is not reflected in legislation. The legal requirement is to cover the content of the programmes of study for years 3 to 6 by the end of key stage 2.

(DfE, 2013c p.6)

Additionally, there are many other examples in the documents which are guidance only. This means that schools have the opportunity to make their own choices about when they teach curriculum content, and what their expectations might be for children attainment at any stage, and therefore the progress they might make. What schools are aware of is, that for core subjects, they will be held accountable for the outcomes of assessments in Year 6.

As we have just illustrated, the national curriculum is presented as only part of any school's curriculum, so schools can enhance the statutory content to make their curriculum fitted to their particular context.

It is up to individual schools, or trusts where they seek consistency across their settings, to make decisions about their curriculum design, assessment and mapping of progress.

REFLECTIVE QUESTIONS

- How is your statutory curriculum structured and sequenced?
- How is it broadened and enhanced?
- Which subjects or other aspects are assessed and tracked?
- How are judgements made as to how well the children are doing? What are the criteria for attainment and progress?
- What are the expectations of progress in every area of the school curriculum?

ACCOUNTABILITY

We have emphasised previously how accountability measures have a significant impact on the decisions the schools make. Accountability for schools works in two key ways: annual pupil outcomes as measured by statutory tests and assessments in core subjects and the inspection regime. The following sections provide some detail.

STATUTORY ASSESSMENTS

SUMMATIVE OUTCOMES

Although this is a book about progress, summative outcomes for core subjects (DfE, 2022) have a significant impact on how schools structure their curriculum, and what they choose to measure and track progress. This is because they will be held accountable, through league tables and Ofsted inspections, not just for summative outcomes but also for the progress that children make between statutory assessments. These standardised assessment tests (SATs) are particularly beneficial for the government, and for Ofsted, as it means a range of statistics can be explored remotely, showing not just summative outcomes but also the progress that pupils in individual schools have made. The data also extend to the analysis of outcomes against a range of criteria, such as gender, disadvantage and special educational needs and disability (SEND). It can also show patterns between schools with differing characteristics, over LA areas and over time (DfE, 2022).

Table 3.2 outlines the statutory assessments for the school year 2023–24. Key Stage 1 tests and assessments became optional from the year 2023/2024, but as materials remain available, many schools may continue to administer these for their own purposes. Baseline assessments became statutory from 2021/22. It is emphasised on pages 5 and 6 that the EYFS profile is to be used to support transition into Key Stage 1 and is not an accountability measure (DfE, 2023d).

Table 3.2 Statutory summative assessments

Assessment		Timing
Baseline	Mathematics	Within six weeks of starting in reception
	Language	
	Communication	
	Literacy	
Early Years Foundation Profile		Reception year
Phonics check		Year 1 Year 2 if below the standard in Year 1
Multiplication table check		Year 4
Key Stage 2	Grammar, punctuation and spelling test	Year 6
	Reading test	
	Mathematics tests 1 and 2	
	Teacher assessments in reading, writing, mathematics and science	

The Standards and Testing Agency (STA, online undated) is responsible for developing these assessments and have these responsibilities:

- developing and implementing assessment policy to measure pupils' progress in primary schools, including assessment arrangements for pupils working below the standard of the national curriculum tests;

- delivering national curriculum assessment cycles, including the development and delivery of tests at Key Stage 1 (KS1) and KS2, as well as the phonics screening check, multiplication tables check and reception baseline assessment;

- supporting schools to administer tests, checks and assessments;

- setting and maintaining test standards;

- managing the submission and moderation of teacher assessment.

A technical guide (DfE, 2023g) explains to schools, in detail, how these assessments are converted into numerical data that can be statistically analysed to demonstrate attainment and progress. Measuring progress from Key Stage 1–2 could be argued as relatively straightforward in terms of producing numerical data, when the measuring instruments take the same form; however, this document shows that even if we take a reductionist approach to assessment content, it becomes complex.

PROGRESS MEASURES

Primary tests and assessments were cancelled in 2019/20 and 2020/21 due to COVID-19. As a result of this, and the changes to statutory assessments in reception and Key Stage 1, in 2023–24, schools are in a period of change regarding progress as measured by statutory means. There will therefore be no progress measures altogether in the years 2023/2024 and 2024/2025. However, the government intend to return to the use of Key Stage 1 outcomes, as before, to measure and report on pupil progress for Year 6 pupils in the years 2025/26 and 2026/27. In the future, government statistics will chart the progress of children in schools who took the baseline assessment in 2021/22 from that assessment to their Year 6 outcomes in 2027/28, rather than from Key Stage 1 to Key Stage 2. A summary of the assessments used to measure progress appears in Table 3.3.

Table 3.3   Government progress measures

Reception baseline	Year 2 SATs	Year 6	Progress measure
		2023/24	
		2024/25	
	2021/22	2025/26	KS1→KS2
	2022/23	2026/27	KS1→KS2
2021/22		2027/28	Baseline→KS2

As you will recall from the McIntosh Commission for Assessment Without Level (CAWL) report (DfE, 2015c), these data are aimed at gathering summary and comparable data for government, LAs the public and school leaders. It is important to recognise the purpose and limits of these data for schools. We earlier outlined the challenges produced in developing assessments against the new curriculum in 2014 and the messages about separation between these assessments and in school tracking. We should recognise that to measure, analyse and present children's outcomes and progress nationally through testing and assessment in a way that is practical is bound to cover just a fraction of what has been taught, and what children have achieved. Choices must be made by government as well as schools when it comes to pupil assessment.

At this point, it can be helpful to consider some questions we might pose about decisions made, and reflect on some of the implications. Some of these questions could also be applied, not just to government but also to school decision-making. Look in the box for the questions, reflect first, before going on to read about some of the implications you might, or might not, have thought about.

REFLECTIVE QUESTIONS

- What curriculum is the basis for assessment?
- What aspects of the urriculum will be assessed?
- How will instruments to make judgements against that standard be constructed?
- What standard of attainment against that curriculum will be established and how shall they be captured?
- How will instruments to make judgements against that standard be constructed?
- What benchmarks will be used to measure progress? What if pupils have different starting points?
- What standard measure of progress between the two points will be agreed?

SOME IMPLICATIONS OF REFLECTIVE QUESTIONS

WHAT CURRICULUM IS THE BASIS FOR ASSESSMENT?

Only the national curriculum for KS1 and KS2 can be used, as this is the only curriculum that all children nationally must statutorily be taught. This curriculum, as we have seen from Chapter 1, has a range of assumptions about what is of value built into it.

- What aspects of the curriculum will be assessed?

    - It is a substantial curriculum, and it would agued as impractical to gather data on the whole of it. The original version the national curriculum carried with it a comprehensive assessment system, but this idea was soon dropped due to its impracticability (ref). The core subjects of English, mathematics and science are the only subjects to be assessed for national statistics, and science does not have the same status as English and mathematics as a core subject. Science only has a teacher assessment and no tests; this may have implications for in school assessment and tracking.

- What standard of attainment against that curriculum will be established and how shall they be captured?

    - The standards criteria, as derived from the national curriculum content, and as measured by tests or by teacher assessments, are decided by current government policy. They decide what they think is of most value within the curriculum, and what might be expected in terms of outcomes for Year 6 pupils, and this may change over time and changes in government.

    - Qualitative data, such as that gathered through teachers using assessment frameworks, must be converted to quantitative data in order to make statistical comparisons. This is done by grouping children into 'levels' of attainment: for example, working towards expectations, at expectations or exceeding expectations.

- How will instruments to make judgements against that standard be constructed?

    - This is the work of STA (see above), and they work with very clear guidelines to produce fair and accurate assessments, although they are not without challenge (ref).

- What benchmarks will be used to measure progress? And what if pupils have different starting points?

    - The standard at least two different points in a pupil's journey through primary school must be set. Measurements taken in the same way, in the same form, increases the validity and reliability of progress measures.

    - It has been decided to use the new baseline assessment through to KS2 to measure progress; yet these data are in different forms and gathered in a very different way.

    - Not all assessments are designed to measure progress but are a check point for learning material seen as fundamental to the broader curriculum area, such as phonics for reading and writing and times tables for mathematics.

- What standard measure of progress between the two points will be agreed?
  - This may not be an absolute measurement applied all children. Must lower attainers make more progress to achieve the standard in Year 6?

The DfE publish Key Stage 2 data in the form of tables, including progress data, at school, LA, regional and national levels (DfE, 2019b), although here was an interruption of SATs for the years 2019/20 and 2021/22 as previously stated, and school level data for 2021/22 was only shared with Ofsted, academy trusts, LAs and the schools themselves. Any member of the public can search for individual school data on the 'Compare School performance' website (DfE online), but perhaps the strongest driver of school's response is the inspectorate.

OFSTED

Ofsted is described as a non-ministerial department, and as such should be protected from political interference. Its role is to provide information to government, helping to form and evaluate policy. Reporting directly to parliament, one of its key responsibilities is inspection of schools, including academies. The 2022–27 strategy lists the raising standards as their first strategic priority (Ofsted, online).

Their inspection responsibilities and activities are laid out in a number of documents which are regularly updated and are summarised in Table 3.4.

Table 3.4   Ofsted inspection documentation

Types of school inspections (Ofsted, undated)	This confirms that all schools will be periodically inspected and that they will receive a grade or have a previous grade confirmed. If there is a concern, and that could include poor outcomes for pupils, inspection may come sooner than previously expected. The government blog in June 2023 (Ofsted, 2023a) gives the detail to help schools know when they will next be inspected.
Education inspection framework (Ofsted, 2023b)	The framework is brief and relies on the detail in the handbook below. It does, however, list the grading scale: outstanding, good, requires improvement and inadequate.
School inspection handbook (Ofsted, 2023c)	The handbook refers to progress a number of times, and it is worth looking at exactly what it says in this regard in Table 3.5. The progress that pupils make, using data available to Ofsted in advance, as well as what they see during the inspection, will inform the judgements made.
School monitoring handbook (Ofsted, 2022)	This handbook comes to bear when school are to receive monitoring visits as a result of the grading following a full inspection or because of a 'requires improvement' grading at the last two. They note here that a well-sequenced curriculum is a key focus in schools that improve.
Inspecting the curriculum (Ofsted, 2019)	Ofsted will also carry out curriculum inspections, and this is school's opportunity to show progress in foundation subjects and science. In the next chapter, we take the opportunity to explore an Ofsted report on history as an example of possible issues around the measurement of progress in foundation subjects.

The inspection handbook is the most detailed document, and this outlines very clearly what inspectors will be looking for. Table 3.5 draws extracts pertaining to progress from the document and outlines some implications for schools. Note that Ofsted does not demand data in any particular form, and this emphasises that schools are able to make their own decisions about how and what they track in terms of pupil progress. As we discussed earlier, the CAWL report (DfE, 2015c) emphasised that school tracking systems are for schools to design and that they should not be over influenced by statutory assessment. In the previous chapter, we gave examples of reports from the National Association of Head Teachers in 2017 and the National Foundation for Educational Research in 2018 which stressed that schools were not heeding to this guidance. This is an opportunity to reflect on whether this is still the case, and how schools have since responded and made decisions about tracking progress through the school years.

Table 3.5 Ofsted handbook references to progress

Section	What the handbook says	Implications
16	It will not ask schools to provide: • predictions of attainment and progress scores; • performance and pupil-tracking information.	Schools do not have to provide tracking or target setting data during the inspection.
58	An outline of what information they analyse as a 'risk assessment', eg: • data from the DfE (eg, progress, attainment, attendance and exclusion data).	Ofsted can access the school inspection summary data report (ISDR) (Ofsted, 2023d) for a school they are preparing to inspect. This includes how they compare with other schools in the progress they make between Key Stage 1 and Key Stage 2. This report does not give detailed data – rather it flags up concerns where a school is performing less well than others.
213	A summary of what the inspectors will use to consider progress for children. It says: • This will include their view of how pupils are progressing through the curriculum, and their view on schemes of work or other long-term planning (in whatever form subject leaders normally use them).	Note that progress here is characterised as 'progress through the curriculum' and that there is a focus on long-term planning. This is not about progress measures between key stages. This suggests what is being assessed and tracked here is attainment on a curriculum that is planned as a scheme or a sequence. In this model, attainment against specific curriculum content, at specific, planned stages in the curriculum will form the 'standard'. Earlier, we mentioned age-related expectations (AREs) and we will come back to this when we are looking at school practices in the next chapter. Age is not mentioned here, but curriculum is. We will argue for referring to curriculum-related

Table 3.5 (Continued)

Section	What the handbook says	Implications
		expectations (CREs), rather than AREs, as they will be unique to the setting, rather than nationally agreed for any particular year group.
214	All pupils, particularly disadvantaged pupils and those with SEND: • acquire the knowledge and cultural capital they need to succeed in life; • make progress, in that they know more, remember more and are able to do more. They are learning what is intended in the curriculum; • produce work of high quality; • achieve well in national tests and examinations, where relevant; • are being prepared for their next stage of education, training or employment at each stage of their learning, including whether pupils in sixth form are ready for the next stage and are going on to appropriate, high-quality destinations; • are able to read to an age-appropriate level and fluency (if not, they will be incapable of accessing the rest of the curriculum, and they will fall rapidly behind their peers).	The curriculum focus is emphasised once more in this section which is quoted in full. It refers to national assessments and readiness for the next stage. Only with regard to reading is age mentioned, and this is in relation to accessing the curriculum. There is no guidance or reference point for 'age appropriate' in this context but could relate to accessibility of the school-designed sequenced curriculum.
221	Inspectors will not look at non-statutory internal progress and attainment data on inspections of schools.	These data are for schools to design and use, not for accountability, although they will want to know that schools are effectively monitoring and acting what they know about pupil attainment progress.
249	Inspectors will look at pupils' work. Work scrutiny will help inspectors to form a view of whether pupils know more and can do more, and whether the knowledge and skills they have learnt are well sequenced and have developed incrementally.	Progress through the curriculum will be inferred from children's work – this will be triangulated with joint lesson visits (section 247) and discussions with staff and pupils (245, 246). This could help schools to avoid becoming too focussed on written evidence in children's books, but it is easy to see how providing different sorts of evidence may present a challenge for schools.

(Continued)

Table 3.5 (Continued)

Section	What the handbook says	Implications
338	When used effectively, assessment helps pupils to embed knowledge and use it fluently and assists teachers in producing clear next steps for pupils. However, assessment is too often carried out in a way that creates unnecessary burdens for staff and pupils. It is therefore important that leaders and teachers understand its limitations and avoid misuse and overuse.	A further reference, indirectly to sequencing, when it talks about 'next steps'. It emphasises unnecessary work for teachers, and the limitations of assessment, cautioning against misuse and overuse.
340 and 341	Collecting data can also create an additional workload for leaders and staff. Inspectors will look at whether schools' collections of attainment or progress data are proportionate, represent an efficient use of school resources, and are sustainable for staff. The Teacher Workload Advisory Group's report, 'Making data work', (DfE, 2019d) recommends that school leaders should not have more than 2 or 3 data collection points a year, and that these should be used to inform clear actions. Schools choosing to use more than 2 or 3 data collection points a year should have clear reasoning for: • what interpretations and actions are informed by the frequency of collection; • the time taken to set assessments, collate, analyse and interpret the data; • the time taken to then act on the findings.	A direct reference to tracking through regular data collections. Again, it cautions against additional workload which is not purposeful in terms of attainment or progress.
389	Inspectors will take account of all the judgements made across the evaluation schedule. In particular, they should consider: • the extent to which leaders and staff plan, design and implement the Early Years curriculum; • the extent to which the curriculum and care practices meet the needs of the range of children who attend, particularly any children with SEND;	These two sections should help schools to maintain both a broad view of elements of attainment and progress. In particular: • the importance of effective curriculum planning in the Early Years; • the needs of children with SEND; • progress over time from starting points; • readiness for the next stage;

Table 3.5 *(Continued)*

Section	What the handbook says	Implications
	• the progress all children make in their learning and development relative to their starting points and their readiness for the next stage of their education; • children's personal, social and emotional development, including whether they feel safe and are secure, stimulated and happy.	• the importance of children being cared for, safe, secure and happy; • schools should then ensure that assessment practice meets these considerations.
391	Inspectors will look at children's learning and development over time. They will ascertain how well the curriculum is meeting children's needs. This will be evident in the extent to which children know and remember more of the intended curriculum. Inspectors need to make careful inferences about children's current progress by drawing together evidence from a range of sources.	

4

PROGRESS THROUGH PRIMARY SCHOOL

KEY WORDS: ASSESSMENT; BENCHMARKS; CORE SUBJECTS; FOUNDATION SUBJECTS; NON-ACADEMIC SKILLS; TRACKING

TRACKING PROGRESS FROM RECEPTION TO YEAR 6

We might start by looking at the language used to describe the outcomes of KS2 statutory assessment: for tests in reading, GPS and mathematics and for statutory teacher assessment in writing and science. These are the only examples of 'age-related expectations' (AREs) or a nationally applied standard measure that might influence us when we start thinking about what children in the other year groups might be expected to achieve, and how we might structure systems to track pupil progress. However, we will see that only in two cases, writing and science, characterised through a descriptive framework, or rubric, and that is because it applies to a teacher assessment. Other expectations are based on a score in a test. This means that we do not have an example of a rubric to support assessment of reading, or mathematics, and certainly no other curriculum subject areas. Where we do have an assessment framework, we can see that the term 'mastery', as originally suggested, is not used and that 'levels' of attainment are reduced to a maximum of three, described in each case as set out in Table 4.1.

Notice the different descriptors used across the assessments, and across documentation. Perhaps the most significant variation is to be found when pupil attainment is variously described as outside the standard. In the three examples where children have yet to be awarded the standard, we could argue that conceptually, there is a difference between 'emerging' and 'working towards', and 'not met'. Perhaps 'not *yet* met' might better mirror the first two examples so that parents and carers know that their children are still recognised as moving forward, and the prospect of meeting the standard might still be in sight. 'Not met' seems rather to signal a failure at the end of this key stage, and with it, questions as to what happens for them as they move to a new year group, and a new age-related 'expected standard'. The language signals an important distinction if we recall the purpose of the new curriculum and its emphasis on assessment without levels. As Tim Oates explained: the notion was that every child, with support, can master the curriculum content. We might ask – is the 'standard' one that we aim for all to meet? The target the government sets in 2023 is for 90% of children to meet the standard across the subjects, suggesting that only in very specific circumstances would they not.

If we look further down the table, then we see even further language variation. The term 'achieving' or 'meeting' rather than 'working' seems to convey a subtly different message, again signalling either something done and dusted or simply a point in an ongoing journey. 'Achieving' or 'meeting' sounds like a measure of attainment of final and complete, while 'working at' something more active and ongoing. Conceptually, perhaps not an enormous difference, but perhaps indicative of how language choice can change our view of what we are looking at, and what conclusions we make about children when we make these assessments. There is a further difference, which perhaps links back to the original difficulty in

Table 4.1 *The language of statutory assessment*

Descriptor	Source example	Tests				Teacher assessments			
		Phonics test	Tables test	Mathematics tests	Reading test	GPS test	Writing assessment	Science assessment	Early learning goals
Working towards the expected standard				✓	✓	✓	✓		
Has not met the expected standard	Information for parents KS2 results 2023 (STA, 2023c)							✓	
Emerging	EYFS Profile 2024 handbook								✓
Working at the expected standard		✓	✓	✓	✓	✓	✓	✓	
Meeting the level of development expected	EYFS Profile 2024 handbook								✓

Achieving at the higher standard	Provisional attainment statistics 2022 (DfE, 2022)		✓	✓	✓	✓	
Working above the expected standard	Information for parents KS2 results 2023 (STA, 2023c)		✓	✓	✓		
Working at greater depth within the expected standard	Teacher assessment frameworks (DfE, 2018b)					✓	
Achieving a high score	Provisional attainment statistics 2022 (DfE, 2022)		✓	✓	✓		

removing levels when a range of attainment might be obvious. It could be seen in the use of 'higher standard' as opposed to 'working at greater depth within the expected standard'. When referring to a higher standard, it suggests moving out of the expected standard altogether – 'greater depth' suggests a quality that is possible within the original standard and fits much better with the original idea of mastery for all.

However, this notion of 'greater depth' only appears in the teacher assessment framework for writing. As part of a set of descriptive criteria, it is designed for teachers to make sense of and categorise what are essentially qualitative data. Science has the only other teacher assessment, and there is just one set of criteria for that – for working at the standard. As far as this notion of 'greater depth' is concerned, we only have what that means in terms of writing for the end of a key stage. You may remember from the previous chapter that the advice was to be cautious about making direct links between statutory and in-school assessment, since they are for different purposes, and different audiences. Yet this descriptor is not uncommon in school tracking systems, and for curriculum content in all year groups, and for other subjects than writing. Any framework adopting this language does not have a standardised model to follow in any area of the curriculum but writing, and this is limited to two-year groups. (Although the KS1 statutory assessment is discontinued, the assessment framework remains available for schools to use.) This does not necessarily mean that this language should not be used in other curriculum contexts, but whatever descriptors might be used for characterising children's attainment and progress, there needs to be agreement and clarity about what they mean. It has to be decided exactly what we expect from children in different year groups in terms of attainment, and what progress looks like in terms of any framework used. Crucially, we need to acknowledge our rationale around any links we make between statutory and in-school assessment and progress tracking.

PROGRESS THROUGH THE YEARS: SCHOOL TRACKING SYSTEMS

This next section looks at some of the ways that schools use to measure and track pupil progress, by addressing the reflective questions.

REFLECTIVE QUESTIONS

- What choices have been made about setting up a tracking system?
- What language does the tracking system use?
- What do the data represent and what do they show the class teacher or middle or senior leaders? What don't they show?
- What data are collected, and how often are data collected and recorded?
- How are the benchmarked criteria chosen at each data point and are these derived?
    - Would you describe these criteria as 'age-related expectations' (AREs) or 'curriculum-related expectations' (CREs)?
    - How do they represent progress through a well-sequenced curriculum?
- Is attainment 'levelled'? At two or more 'levels'? What could inform the criteria for these?

(Continued)

- How does the system characterise progress, through the year, and from year to year, when each year covers discrete curriculum content?
- How can the data be used to promote, as well as measure, progress?
- How can the data be used to support transition between key stages and different curricula?
- How is target setting used, and what is its purpose?

As you look through the questions, keep in mind the measured benchmarks at the end of key stages, the Commission for Assessment Without Levels (CAWL) report extracts in Chapter 2, and any notes that you took, and reflect on earlier discussions about knowledge and curriculum in the first chapter. A little later, in Figure 4.2, you will see a graphical representation of all the things that need to be considered when setting up an efficient an effective tracking system.

BENCHMARKS

We have talked in the earlier sections a good deal about attainment at different points in children's time at primary school. An emphasis throughout has been put on the importance of a sequenced curriculum, with Ofsted cautioning about simply hitting data points and that attainment against a well-sequenced curriculum is progress. Becky Allen (2018) has an interesting blog on the notion of measuring progress between two measurable points. Although also aimed at secondary education, it acknowledges the value of tests and assessments as invaluable teacher tools for teaching, but queries whether we are actually measuring progress at all. She particularly raises the issue about what it tells us about progress from one test to another.

The curriculum subject documents are useful in drawing our attention to the notion of progress, not just attainment at key points but knowledge building, moving forward from one point to the next in a cohesive way. This we might describe as progress. As long as the curriculum is well sequenced, and the content is mastered at each stage, progress is achieved. This seems to fit well with the ideals that underpin the 2014 curriculum.

However, it has become standard and accepted practice that during each child's primary school journey, the school will set a number of points at which data will be collected. The end of the key stage is an obvious point, as this is the point where the expectation is that a whole curriculum will have been taught. The Key Stage 2 final assessments are felt to carry high stakes due to their function as an accountability measure. Similarly, the end of Key Stage 1 outcomes, and in the future the baseline, are identified as starting points for progress accountability. These assessments, reduced as they are to some very specified outcomes in core subjects, have the potential to become over significant in terms of tracking progress, eclipsing the wish to measure success and progress for all children, in any year group, in a wide range of subject-based and other areas of learning. Points in between can tend to focus on aspects of the curriculum which are to be measured at the end of Key Stage 2, to the exclusion of the foundation subjects, and other aspects of the wider curriculum. Benchmarks, therefore, are often set around data collection focussing on key learning in English and mathematics, and to a lesser extent, science. Data will usually be collected two or three times a year and will cover curriculum content drawn from the national curriculum, guided by the non-statutory guidance on what might be taught in particular year groups. The sequencing of the core subject's curriculum will this be constructed through a series of curriculum extracts and referred to variously as Key Learning, Key Objectives or Age-Related Expectations (AREs).

Schools could:

- scrutinise the curriculum, and lay out the content in some sort of sequential order through the year groups;

- follow the structure provided through their MAT or subject hub;

- apply the system within purchased tests;

- buy in a tracking system; or

- apply a combination of these.

An example of a typical core subject tracking spreadsheet can be found in Table 4.3. This example is for an end of key stage year group, but as noted previously, there are no nationally agreed expectations of children of different ages. Although guided by the layout of the document itself, it is up to schools when they teach content, and perhaps therefore these expectations might better be described as curriculum-related expectations. The school will decide to teach certain curriculum content in Year 3, for example, and attainment against this content is what will be assessed. We will come back to this tracking sheet a little later.

PROGRESS IN FOUNDATION SUBJECTS

Planning for progress in foundation subjects is relieved of the pressure of Key Stage 2 standardised assessment tests (SATs) and could be said to offer more freedom to schools in curriculum sequencing and assessing attainment. There is much detail in the national curriculum documents about the content, and to a degree, the sequence of learning, of core subjects, and this can be used to provide the basis of designing a curriculum which supports progress and its related expectations of children as they move through the school. This is not, however, the case in terms of foundation subjects. Although there are no statutory assessments, schools can still be held accountable by Ofsted and the agency may gather information through both their full and curriculum inspections. In the handbook, a clear focus on sequencing and developing knowledge and skills is identified:

> the extent to which the school's curriculum. . . . is planned and sequenced so that the end points that it is building towards are clear and that pupils develop the knowledge and skills, building on what has been taught before, to be able to reach those end points.

> (Ofsted, 2023e para 227)

We have emphasised the, sometimes negative, impact of Ofsted on curriculum, assessment and progress tracking of core subjects, but it can be instructive to look at foundation subject reports and research reviews published between 2021 and 2023. Often, subject associations or other bodies will provide a response to reports and research reviews, and it is worth also referring to those. They may not all agree, but these may also help you, especially if not a specialist, to focus your thinking about progress in specific subject areas. Although each report is about a specific curriculum subject, a number of key points can often be drawn, which could apply to other subjects and can contribute to a cohesive view of the role of curriculum in supporting progress. You will notice that the same elements supporting progress recur, specifically:

- a well-sequenced curriculum.

- an understanding of teaching and assessing the different domains of knowledge within the subjects.

- the identification of specific learning objectives and assessments designed to support knowledge building and future learning in all domains.

As examples, we have drawn out a few key points drawn from two subject reports and a research review from 2023.

Ofsted recently reported on history (Ofsted, 2023e) and geography (Ofsted, 2023f).

History

- A well-planned, sequenced curriculum, covering both substantive and disciplinary knowledge is imperative for progress.

- Curriculum plans should identify the most important content and concepts to be taught to support future learning.

- Curriculum themes which can be developed in terms of complexity is an approach that will support progress over a variety of topic content.

- Effective assessment is built on a strong curriculum and developmental, specific and rich learning objectives which support future learning.

- Important knowledge that every pupil needs to master at points in the curriculum needs to be identified; a focus on isolated facts and superficial skills is not effective in promoting progress.

Geography

- Knowledge building across topics is important.

- Areas of knowledge were identified as substantive, disciplinary and procedural.

- Disciplinary knowledge was identified as the weaker area of curriculum thinking than substantive, and procedural the weakest.

- The report cautions against 'simplistic' knowledge including lists of disconnected facts.

- Curriculum planning should take account of concepts as well as topic content.

- Assessment of attainment and progress should include disciplinary and procedural knowledge as well as substantive progress.

Art

A research review for art was published in 2023 (Ofsted, 2023g).

- A clear indication of the domains of knowledge that can be built over time. In this case, three are listed: practical (technical proficiency), theoretical (cultural and contextual) and disciplinary.

- Summative assessment is clear about the knowledge being assessed.

- It reiterates that the curriculum forms the model for progression.

We would also recommend another book in this series, Nasreen Majid's *Essential Subject Knowledge for Primary Teaching* (2023), which covers all subjects on the national curriculum as well as PSHE (personal, social and health education), RE (religious education) and sustainability and climate change. This, together with the curriculum itself, the Ofsted documents and subject association websites and resources, can help to support your thinking on progression and the construction of a well-sequenced curriculum grounded in an understanding of progression in each subject.

PROGRESS IN WIDER OR NON-ACADEMIC SKILLS

We have thought a good deal about academic subjects within the curriculum, but to focus only on these, especially without identifying common skills, risks neglecting other aspects of pupil progress. It is easy to make assumptions that learning in these areas will occur quite naturally in the course of learning the subject curriculum, but this may not be the case. We have already noted the agreement that curriculum should include content broader than academic subjects. What does this mean?

Table 4.2 extracts briefly some the content in the two curriculum documents which identify areas outside those explicitly contained within the primary academic subjects or that recur across subjects. Notice how in the Early Years curriculum some of these are centre stage, as principles or as assessment areas, whereas in the national curriculum, they appear in the preamble to or included within the subject content which will necessarily form the focus for teaching, assessment and progress tracking. Strong messages within the Early Years curriculum which are not explicitly taken forward into Key Stage 1 are the notions of individuality and independence. This is a good opportunity to reflect on the forms of knowledge and curriculum explored in Part 1.

Table 4.2   Wider curriculum content

EYFS	National curriculum
Overarching principles: Every child ...is a unique child, who is constantly learning and can be resilient, capable, confident and self-assured.	2.2 **The school curriculum** comprises all learning and other experiences that each school plans for its pupils. The national curriculum forms one part of the school curriculum.

Table 4.2 (Continued)

EYFS	National curriculum
...can learn to be strong and independent through positive relationships (p. 6).	2.5 Schools are also free to include other subjects or topics of their choice in planning and designing their own programme of education. 3.2 **The national curriculum** is just one element in the education of every child. There is time and space in the school day and in each week, term and year to range beyond the national curriculum specifications. The national curriculum provides an outline of core knowledge around which teachers can develop exciting and stimulating lessons to promote the development of pupils' knowledge, understanding and skills as part of the wider school curriculum.
Prime areas • communication and language (CLL) • physical development • personal, social and emotional development (p.8).	2.1 Every state-funded school must offer a curriculum which is balanced and broadly based and which: • promotes the spiritual, moral, cultural, mental and physical development of pupils at the school and of society, and • prepares pupils at the school for the opportunities, responsibilities and experiences of later life.
CLL The development of children's spoken language underpins all seven areas of learning and development.	6.1 Teachers should develop pupils' spoken language, reading, writing and vocabulary as integral aspects of the teaching of every subject.
PSED Children's personal, social and emotional development (PSED) is crucial for children to lead healthy and happy lives and is fundamental to their cognitive development (p.8). PSED Early Learning Goals Self-regulation Managing self Building relationships (p.12).	2.5 All schools should make provision for personal, social, health and economic education (PSHE), drawing on good practice.

(Continued)

Table 4.2 (Continued)

EYFS	National curriculum
Characteristics of effective teaching and learning, creating and thinking critically – children have and develop their own ideas, make links between ideas and develop strategies for doing things.	6.2 Spoken language [Pupils should] ...learn to justify ideas with reasons; ask questions to check understanding; develop vocabulary and build knowledge; negotiate; and evaluate and build on the ideas of others.
	Statutory requirements maintain attention and participate actively in collaborative conversations, staying on topic and initiating and responding to comments.
	...use spoken language to develop understanding through speculating, hypothesising, imagining and exploring ideas (p.17).
	Creativity is identified in art and design (176, 177); computing (178); design and technology (180, 183); and music (187).

Shipton and Bermingham (2018) wrote a clear summary of what they call non-academic skills for the House of Parliament in 2018. They point to a range of studies that show the impact of non-academic skills on academic success, life chances, mental and physical health and wellbeing. They acknowledge the challenge of classifying these skills, particularly on account of overlapping not just with each other and with academic subjects. However, they do suggest a list, although they do not claim it to be all encompassing. Figures 4.1 sets these out. Of course, some of them are more likely to occur within academic subjects, but we can set up activities designed to demand specific skills both during subject lessons and as lessons in themselves too. Just as we categorise academic learning through subjects, to promote progress in these skills, it helps to identify them, teach and provide opportunities for them to develop. To measure attainment and progress, as for the academic subjects, we will need to set indicators, criteria or rubrics for success, and if we want to view this in terms of progress, we will need to construct these into a model for progression. To gather assessment data, we can use many of the formative and summative approaches we use for those academic subjects, such as questioning, observing, peer and self-assessment, and explore in more detail with Early Years practitioners how they assess their children's progress in the prime areas, particular CLL and PSED.

▬ REFLECTIVE QUESTIONS ▬

- What non-academic or wider skills might be important for pupil progress?
- Which ones might be the most relevant for the pupils in your school?
- Does your school assess and track progress in any of these areas?
- Can you start to imagine what a progression model in those skills might look like?
- How might you measure attainment and progress?

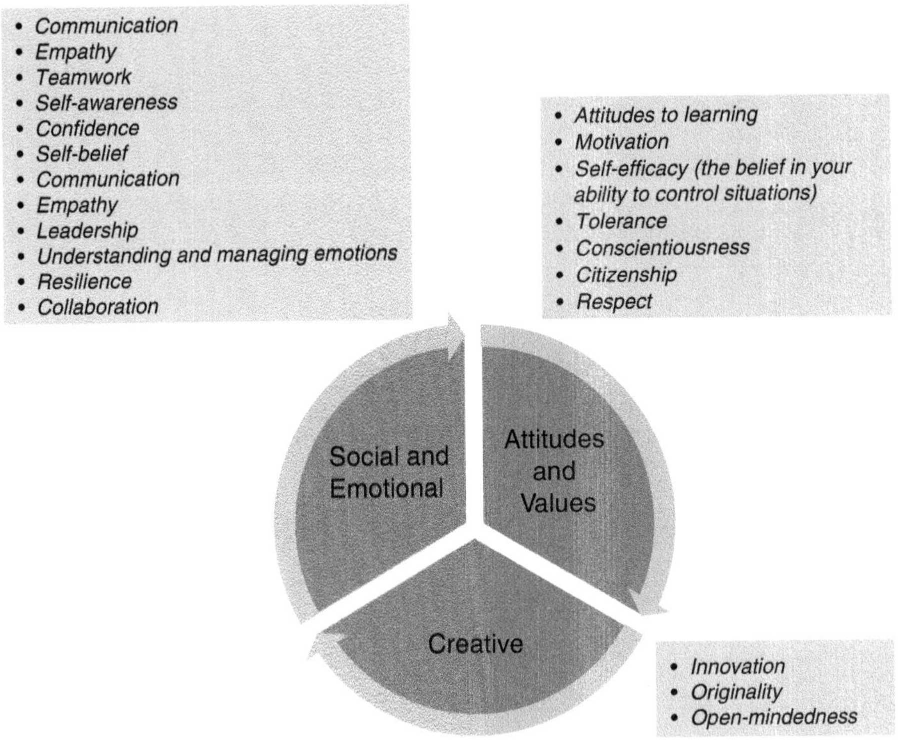

Figure 4.1 Non-academic skills (Shipton and Bermingham, 2018)

TRACKING GRIDS

A little earlier, we referred to Table 4.3 and you will have noticed that assessment levels of 1, 2 and 3 are recorded. Decisions have been made in this instance about how the expectations of attainment might be characterised, as well as how to measure them. The language to describe attainment and the persistent notion of 'levels' may have unconsidered effects on the way we think about attainment and progress as we saw when discussing Table 4.1. Looking back again at Becky Allen's blog, if a child is judged as exceeding expectations in one set of assessments, but only meeting expectations in the next, is that progress? How helpful are these 'levels' in tracking progress, rather than informing planning and teaching to the next round of curriculum expectations? Importantly, schools must be sure that any attainment descriptor is fully understood by all who are working with it and agree on what progress looks like from assessment to assessment, and from year to year.

Schools may choose to take different routes – this is what they have been encouraged to do – and in seeking help and resources many will use purchased tracking systems which lay out the objectives for each year group or bought in tests like those the National Foundation for Educational Research (NFER) provide. Some will develop their own systems for assessment, but this represents a significant commitment, and schools may lack the time, money or expertise to do this effectively. Too many data points may add extra workload on to busy teachers and provide little in terms of benefit (DfE, 2019d), and the quality of

Table 4.3   Example of a tracking grid

Year 2 writing key objectives	Susie	Adam	Kirk	Henry	Ana	Amal	Corrine	Greg	Georgia	Hannah	Alex	George	Priscilla	Barney	Noor	Edie	Saul	Freddie	Nina	Tyrone
Break words into phonemes for spelling	1	3	2	2	2	3	2	1	2	2	3	3	2	1	3	1	3	1	2	3
Know some spellings which use variations of standard phonemes	1	2	2	2	2	2	2	1	2	2	3	3	2	1	3	1	3	1	2	3
Use the possessive apostrophe	2	2	2	2	2	2	2	1	2	2	3	3	2	1	3	1	3	1	2	3
Spell some words with contracted forms	1	2	2	2	2	3	2	1	2	2	3	3	2	1	3	1	3	1	2	3
Use suffixes to spell longer words, including -ment, -ness, -less, -ful, -ly	1	3	2	2	2	3	2	1	2	2	3	3	2	1	3	1	3	1	2	3
Form lowercase letters of the correct size relative to one another	2	2	2	2	2	3	2	1	2	2	2	3	3	2	2	2	2	1	2	3
Write capital letters of appropriate size	2	2	2	2	2	3	2	1	2	2	2	3	3	2	3	1	2	1	2	3
Write for different purposes	2	3	2	2	2	3	2	1	3	2	2	3	3	2	3	2	3	1	2	3
Use noun phrases	2	3	3	2	3	3	3	1	3	2	2	3	2	1	3	2	3	2	2	3
Use the four main types of sentence appropriately	2	3	2	2	2	3	2	1	3	2	2	3	3	1	3	2	3	1	2	3
Use present and past tense correctly	2	3	3	2	2	3	2	1	3	2	2	3	3	1	3	2	3	1	2	3
Use some coordinating and subordinating conjunctions	2	3	2	2	2	3	2	1	3	2	2	3	3	1	3	2	3	1	2	3
Use appropriate demarcation punctuation	2	3	2	2	2	3	2	1	3	2	2	3	3	1	3	2	3	1	2	3
Use commas for lists	2	3	2	2	2	3	2	1	3	2	2	3	3	2	3	2	3	1	2	3
Number of Objectives met	10	14	14	14	14	14	14	0	14	14	14	14	14	4	14	7	14	1	14	14
Number of Objectives exceeded	0	9	2	0	1	12	1	0	7	0	5	14	8	0	12	0	12	0	0	14
Overall standard	W	E	M	M	M	E	M	W	E	M	E	E	E	W	E	W	E	W	M	E

Students meeting expectations:	6 students (30%)
Students exceeding expectations:	9 students (45%)
Students meeting or exceeding expectations:	15 students (75%)
Students below expectations:	5 students (25%)

purchased resources may be in doubt. What is important here is that thought has been given to the questions in previous reflective questions and decisions made after careful consideration, understanding both the strengths and limitations of any approach that is taken.

In any event, schools will typically record assessments on some sort of tracking grid. If they construct their own, they may use a spreadsheet software programme or their school management system.

They may look like Tables 4.3 and 4.4. In this example, colour coding is likely to be added, and the language *below expectations, meeting expectations* and *exceeding expectations* used to indicate a 'level' of attainment. This sample grid is a record of teacher assessments of writing for a Year 2 class in February, using a set of criteria drawn from the Year 2 curriculum. Similar tables record assessments in writing, mathematics and science. It is the second of three data points during this school year, against the same criteria. New sets of criteria will be used when the children are in subsequent years. Table 4.4 is a summary from all four subject assessments. Go back to the questions in question 5 and reflect on what the answers might be in this example and the benefits and limitations of a system like this. In particular, consider the impact on pupil progress in core subjects more widely and how such systems can be enhanced or complemented by other ways of tracking progress.

Table 4.4   *Example of an assessment summary*

	Students	Reading	Writing	Maths	Science
	Susie	W	W	W	E
	Adam	E	E	E	E
	Kirk	M	M	M	M
	Henry	M	M	M	M
	Ana	E	M	E	E
	Amal	E	E	E	E
	Corrine	M	M	W	M
	Greg	W	W	W	E
	Georgia	E	E	E	E
	Hannah	M	M	M	M
	Alex	E	E	E	E
	George	E	E	E	E
	Priscilla	M	E	M	E
	Barney	W	W	W	W
	Noor	E	E	E	E
	Edie	E	W	E	E
	Saul	E	E	E	E
	Freddie	W	W	W	W
	Nina	M	M	M	M
	Tyrone	E	E	E	E

(Continued)

Table 4.4 (Continued)

	Students	Reading	Writing	Maths	Science
Below		4	5	5	2
	Meeting	M	M	M	M
	Exceeding	10	9	10	13
Below		20%	25%	25%	10%
	Meeting	M	M	M	M
	Exceeding	50%	45%	50%	65%
ARE or higher		72.7	68.2	68.3%	81.8%

MAKING DECISIONS

The book, so far, has covered a lot of ground; you may have initially thought that some of it is only tangentially relevant to the notion of pupil progress. After all, no one is challenging the idea that pupil progress is a 'good thing' and something that underpins all of what schools do. What we hope is becoming clearer, that is, what progress actually is: what we call knowledge; what we choose to include in our curriculum and the value we put on particular aspects of it; how we sequence and teach that curriculum; and what and how we recognise, measure and track learning so we can promote and recognise progress in its fullest sense.

Some of these decisions are influenced by the accountability measures that schools face, but we should also see that there is scope for autonomy. The national curriculum was never intended to be the whole curriculum, and end of key stage SATs are not the only measure of success. The removal of levels was intended to take away the idea of accelerated progress and carried with it the expectation that all children could master the curriculum. The CAWL report emphasised the distinction between statutory assessment and in-school tracking of progress. Many have cautioned against using the same frameworks to construct and manage their in-school assessment processes and to be wary of purchased resources that fail to recognise this. Of course, core subjects are core subjects for good reason, but schools know that SATs only assess parts of even those subjects and that other areas of the curriculum, both academic and otherwise, enhance or benefit learning in core subjects and produce a better-rounded primary education and better-rounded children ready for the next stage. Ofsted emphasise the limitation of only considering measured data points.

Before moving on to the next chapter, which looks more closely at teachers in the classroom, have a look at Figure 4.2. This graphic attempts to outline the key things to be considered by schools in setting up their systems and processes for tracking pupil progress. The decisions made at this level will have a significant impact on teachers' day-to-day work.

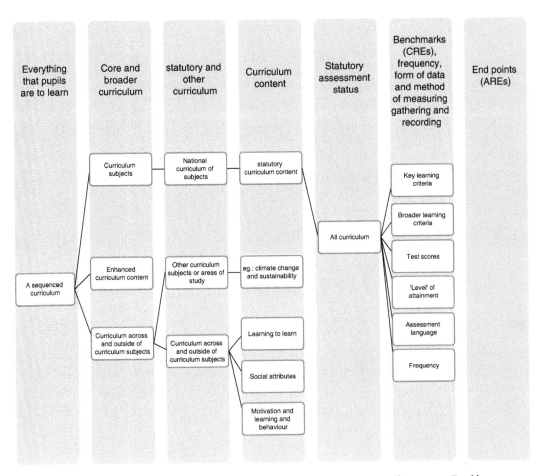

Figure 4.2   Tracking progress

PART 3
PROGRESS IN YOUR CLASSROOM

LINKS TO THE CORE CONTENT FRAMEWORK
(CORE CONTENT AND EARLY CAREER FRAMEWORK)

Standard 1 – 'Set high expectations'

1.3. Teacher expectations can affect pupil outcomes; setting goals that challenge and stretch pupils *(from their starting point)* is essential.

1.4. Setting clear expectations can help communicate shared values that improve classroom and school culture.

Standard 2 – 'Promote good progress'

2.1. Learning involves a lasting change in pupils' capabilities or understanding.

2.2. Prior knowledge plays an important role in how pupils learn; committing some key facts to their long-term memory is likely to help pupils learn more complex ideas.

2.6 *(2.7)*. Where prior knowledge is weak, pupils are more likely to develop misconceptions, particularly if new ideas are introduced too quickly.

Standard 3 – 'Demonstrate good subject and curriculum knowledge'

3.1. A school's curriculum enables it to set out its vision for the knowledge, skills and values that its pupils will learn, encompassing the national curriculum within a coherent wider vision for successful learning.

3.3. Ensuring pupils master foundational concepts and knowledge before moving on is likely to build pupils' confidence and help them succeed.

3.5. Explicitly teaching pupils the knowledge and skills they need to succeed within particular subject areas is beneficial.

3.7. In all subject areas, pupils learn new ideas by linking those ideas to existing knowledge, organising this knowledge into increasingly complex mental models (or 'schemata'); carefully sequencing teaching to facilitate this process is important.

Standard 4 – 'Plan and teach well-structured lessons'

4.2. Effective teachers introduce new material in steps, explicitly linking new ideas to what has been previously studied and learned.

4.5. Explicitly teaching pupils metacognitive strategies linked to subject knowledge, including how to plan, monitor and evaluate, supports independence and academic success.

4.6. Questioning is an essential tool for teachers; questions can be used for many purposes, including to check pupils' prior knowledge, assess understanding and break down problems.

(Continued)

(Continued)

Standard 5 – 'Adapt teaching'

5.2 (5.3). Seeking to understand pupils' differences, including their different levels of prior knowledge and potential barriers to learning, is an essential part of teaching.

5.4. Adaptive teaching is less likely to be valuable if it causes the teacher to artificially create distinct tasks for different groups of pupils or to set lower expectations for particular pupils.

Standard 6 – 'Make accurate and productive use of assessment'

6.1. Effective assessment is critical to teaching because it provides teachers with information about pupils' understanding and needs.

6.2. Good assessment helps teachers avoid being over-influenced by potentially misleading factors, such as how busy pupils appear.

6.3. Before using any assessment, teachers should be clear about the decision that it will be used to support and be able to justify its use.

6.5. High-quality feedback can be written or verbal; it is likely to be accurate and clear, encourage further effort, and provide specific guidance on how to improve.

6.6. Over time, feedback should support pupils to monitor and regulate their own learning.

6.7. Working with colleagues to identify efficient approaches to assessment is important; assessment can become onerous and have a disproportionate impact on workload.

Standard 7 – 'Manage behaviour effectively'

7.6. Pupils are motivated by intrinsic factors (related to their identity and values) and extrinsic factors (related to reward).

7.7. Pupils' investment in learning is also driven by their prior experiences and perceptions of success and failure.

5
FRAMEWORKS FOR PRACTICE

KEY WORDS: APPRAISAL; LEARNING AND DEVELOPMENT; TEACHER'S STANDARDS

Individual teachers as well as those setting out on their career will find themselves in a local context where decisions have been made about curriculum, assessment and attainment and progress, including tracking. They will hopefully have had the chance to contribute to discussions about those decisions, with the view to achieving the very best outcomes for all the children in their school, and for the wider school community, with a sound understanding of statutory demands. The previous chapters have provided an analytical lens through which to view these decisions. This chapter is a practical one, hopefully helping to understand how day-to day-systems and processes and choices about planning and pedagogy can promote pupil progress.

School accountability rests on all those who work in them. School leaders at senior and middle levels will take a whole school strategic view and individual class teachers will work within school plans, procedures and targets to contribute to the outcomes sought in school development plans in order to satisfy those who evaluate them. All teachers, whether school leaders or not, are held to account through a number of statutory frameworks. For beginning teachers, there are two statutory curricula with regard to their own, and pupil, progress: the Initial Teacher Training Core Curriculum Framework (CCF) and Early Career Teachers (ECT) framework. From September 2025, these two frameworks will be combined into the 'Initial Teacher Training and Early Career Framework (ITTECF). For all teachers, and for the purpose of a final assessment for Qualified Teacher Status (QTS), we have the Teachers' Standards.

TEACHERS' STANDARDS

Standard 2: Promote good progress and outcomes by pupils is the focus of this book. The Teachers' Standards in place today were introduced on 1 September 2012 (DfE, 2011b), a development from a set of professional standards developed by the Teacher Development Agency (TDA, 2007), which was closed by the incoming coalition government. The earlier document was a framework to support the stages of teacher development through their career from QTS and beyond. There is a clear reference to pupil progress at every stage, as in the present standards, which are considerably shorter and apply to all teachers. In the QTS threshold list, it was mentioned 7 times, and in the core for qualified teachers, 11 times. However, in no instance is there any detail about what is exactly meant by progress. For example, this appears in both:

> *Plan for progression across the age and ability range for which they are trained, designing effective learning sequences within lessons and across series of lessons and demonstrating secure subject/curriculum knowledge.*

> (TDA, 2007 pp.10, 18)

Making good progress had been at the core of the Labour government's aims for education, but it was often seen in terms of as being as good as, or better than, others. We can see this explicitly in the 'post threshold' teacher list:

Have teaching skills which lead to learners achieving well relative to their prior attainment, making progress as good as, or better than, similar learners nationally.

Of course, the only comparative data which could inform this would be derived from statutory assessment, or from the way pupils progressed through the national curriculum levels in core subjects. The provision of the Assessing Pupil Progress materials mentioned in Part 1 provided a framework to map that from Year 1 to Year 6 (DfE online, n.d.). No such framework exists today.

In the current standards, we see that progress, albeit combined with outcomes, has not only a standard all of its own but also figures large in another: assessment. We have already seen how we cannot talk about progress without talking about assessment, because we have to think about what it is we are making progress in and how we know. It is worth reproducing both standards in full here, highlighting the most relevant sections to be clear about the responsibilities for teachers in terms of pupil progress (our bold):

2. Promote good progress and outcomes by pupils

   - be accountable for pupils' attainment, progress and outcomes.

   - be aware of pupils' capabilities and their prior knowledge, **and plan teaching to build on these.**

   - guide pupils to reflect on the progress they have made and their emerging needs.

   - demonstrate knowledge and understanding of how pupils learn and how this impacts on teaching.

   - encourage pupils to take a responsible and conscientious attitude to their own work and study.

6. Make accurate and productive use of assessment

   - know and understand how to assess the relevant subject and curriculum areas, including statutory assessment requirements.

   - make use of formative and summative assessment to secure pupils' progress.

   - use relevant data to monitor progress, set targets and plan subsequent lessons.

   - give pupils regular feedback, both orally and through accurate marking, and encourage pupils to respond to the feedback.

But are we any clearer about what is meant by pupil progress? Other standards refer to setting goals that stretch and challenge, imparting knowledge and understanding, contributing to the design and provision of an engaging curriculum and teaching effectiveness. We note that it is difficult to talk about progress without assessment, but the reverse is not true – assessment can happen without a focus on progress. It could just be instances of unrelated assessment with no connections and no forward trajectory: what we might call summative assessment and how the end of Key Stage 2 statutory assessments have often come to be viewed, since secondary settings do not use them formatively, although they may use them, possibly combined with other school information, in initial setting of students, especially in English and mathematics. This means that what is applicable within primary settings in any individual case is down to the school's frameworks for progress, with an eye to end of key stage outcomes, any published national progress measures and Ofsted expectations, but with the detail added. The previous chapter explored the challenges that schools must meet in order to construct these frameworks.

FRAMEWORKS FOR TEACHER LEARNING AND DEVELOPMENT

THE ITT CCF AND ECF AND THE NATIONAL PROFESSIONAL QUALIFICATION FOR LEADING TEACHING

From September 2025, the CCF and the ECF will be combined into one framework called the Initial Teacher Training and Early Career Framework (ITTECF). The content of these frameworks will not significantly change. For more information: https://www.gov.uk/government/publications/initial-teacher-training-and-early-career-framework. We notice that the previous standards were clearly linked to teacher development. More was expected of those who had moved up the teaching hierarchy. Now teacher training and development is underpinned through a separate series of frameworks. So, where the standards are a set of qualities that all teachers must demonstrate, the frameworks go into more detail about what teacher must know, understand and practise. The frameworks are the curriculum, and we can think of the standards as a set of assessment criteria. In order for beginning teachers to see how their own progression might develop as they move through their teaching career, we can look further past the ITT core curriculum (DfE, 2019c) and the ECF (DfE, 2019e). There are a number of frameworks for teacher development after the ECT years, but the National Professional Qualification for Leading Teaching (NPQLT) (DfE, 2023a) is the one that focusses on classroom practice most broadly. There are specific National Professional Qualifications for leading English and mathematics, but the others a more focussed on management.

The CCF and ECF, although said to cover five areas of learning for those beginning their teaching careers, or completed their induction as a fully qualified teacher, are presented through the standards, as explained here:

The ITT Core Content Framework – as with the ECF – has been designed to support trainee development in five core areas – behaviour management, pedagogy, curriculum, assessment and professional behaviours. In order to ensure congruence with the eight Teachers' Standards, the ITT Core Content Framework is presented in eight sections. In developing the framework, behaviour management is addressed in high expectations and managing behaviour (S1 and S7); pedagogy is addressed in how pupils learn, classroom practice and adaptive teaching (S2, S4, S5); and curriculum, assessment and professional behaviours are addressed in S3, S6 and S8, respectively.

The NPQLT is laid out as the CCF and ECF as a set of statements for 'learn that' and 'learn how to' covering similar areas.

Scrutinising these documents, we can see that the actual term 'progress' is used rarely (not at all in the NPQLT); however, there are key ideas with the potential to contribute to pupil progress; these follow through and serve to link them together. Reminding ourselves of earlier chapters and what we have discussed about knowledge, learning, curriculum and assessment can we draw out some principles to generate a model for promoting good progress in our everyday classrooms within the statutory and chosen school frameworks?

These seem to emerge from the teacher development curricula, effectively bringing together many of the main themes covered in this book so far:

- Teachers are accountable for pupil progress through their practice in **planning, teaching and assessment**.

- Progress can be mapped through curricula that are coherent and sequenced, incorporating the national curriculum and a wider curriculum **(curriculum planning)**.

- The content of subjects should include themes, concepts and ideas that can be revisited as children progress **(curriculum planning)**.

- Teachers should bring their understanding of how pupils learn to their teaching **(lesson planning, teaching)**.

- New learning is built on prior learning and learning is lasting change **(curriculum and lesson planning, teaching, assessment)**.

- Assessment should be fit for its agreed purpose, and formative assessment should be used to inform target setting, planning and teaching **(assessment)**.

- Children should be involved in their own progress through responding to feedback and reflecting on their own learning **(lesson planning, assessment)**.

- Expectations affect outcomes **(curriculum and lesson planning, teaching, assessment)**.

APPRAISAL/PERFORMANCE MANAGEMENT

Following the award of QTS, teachers are subject to appraisal. The government has provided a model policy (DfE, 2019f). Objectives will be set, and these are likely to include measures of pupil attainment and progress. The model policy states:

> *Objectives and performance management discussions will not be based on teacher generated data and predictions, or solely on the assessment data for a single group of pupils. Objectives can be set in relation to robust assessment data, however, these will not be used in isolation and other factors will also be considered when making decisions about pay progression.*

> (DfE, 2019f pp.7–8)

One of the aims of this book is to encourage readers to expand their view of what progress is, acknowledging the statutory accountabilities to which schools are subject. As you go on to think about the ways in which classroom teachers work to promote progress for all the children in their care, recognise both the strengths and limits of assessment data, in all its forms, and its role in securing the progress you are seeking.

6

IN PRACTICE

KEY WORDS: CURRICULUM; LEARNING BEHAVIOUR; LEARNING OBJECTIVE AND SUCCESS CRITERIA; MENTAL HEALTH AND WELLBEING; MOTIVATION; PARENTS AND CARERS; PLANNING; TARGET SETTING

Having consolidated these ideas into a model for thinking about how they might be put together in schools, this section looks at the detail of a class teacher's practice.

CURRICULUM

So far, we have thought about curriculum largely as a body of content to be taught, and we have emphasised its central function as the core around which pupil progress can be achieved through it structure and how it is operated day to day and over time. Ofsted, in its response to an inspection consultation (Ofsted, 2019d), extended that definition to provide a practical approach to evaluating its success in promoting pupil progress:

- the framework for setting out the aims of a programme of education, including the knowledge and skills to be gained at each stage (intent)

- the translation of that framework over time into a structure and narrative, within an institutional context (implementation)

- the evaluation of what knowledge and skills learners have gained against expectations (impact/ achievement)

This describes a view of the curriculum as a school's interpretation of content, alongside its methods of assessment. In earlier chapters, when discussing the link between curriculum and assessment, we noted that the previous national curriculum had related structured assessment system with criteria for progress built in. Following the introduction of a new curriculum in 2014, we know that schools have had to construct their own systems for assessment, including how they will characterise, measure and track progress, through the year groups, since the key aim is for children to 'master' the curriculum content by a certain end point. We could argue that Ofsted's working definition integrates curriculum and assessment, rather than separates them. You may recall a further Ofsted quote from earlier on the book and here we extend it, as it makes clear the links between not just curriculum and assessment but also pedagogy and progress and how curriculum becomes more than just a list of content, but the progression model, as we suggested earlier:

The curriculum is also distinct from pedagogy, which is how the curriculum is taught. Furthermore, it is distinct from assessment, which is a means of evaluating whether learners are learning/have learnt the intended curriculum, although of course the curriculum and assessment need to work hand in hand. In so doing, the curriculum becomes the progression model [...] Progress should not be defined by hitting the next data point. Rather, if learners attain within a well-sequenced, well-constructed curriculum, they are making progress.

(Ofsted, 2019a p.5)

Clearly, what curriculum is taught, and when, has a major impact on its effectiveness, quite apart from how it is taught. So clarity over curriculum, assessment and teaching are all important and the way they work together even more so as the driver of progress. What does this mean for the class teacher?

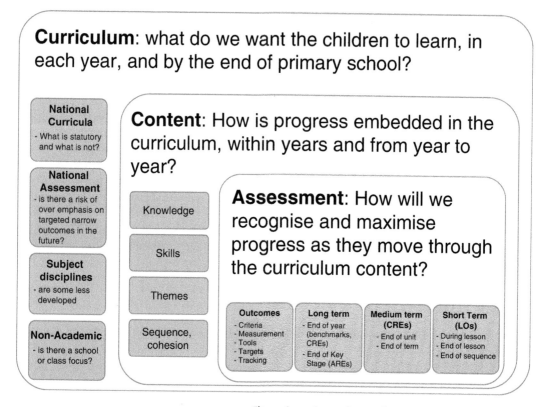

Figure 6.1   Promoting good progress – A curriculum model

Familiarity with the requirements of national curriculum content in all subjects and in other statutory and guidance documentation is essential. This includes not just factual content but concepts, ideas and skills inherent in the subject discipline that form the basis of progress in the subject. This is particularly important in foundation subjects which are less detailed in the national curriculum programmes of study, and we have seen from the Ofsted curriculum reports that this has not always been a priority. Policy and tracking documents and long- and medium-term plans can provide a discussion point for exploring this with mentors. Knowing how the school has interpreted the statutory curriculum in framing a sequenced content for teaching will support planning and teaching, and using and adapting the plans that schools have in place more effectively.

It is important to be aware of any areas of learning outside of the subject-based curriculum that are contained within the school's policies or development plans. These are not just important in themselves, but, as we saw in the note to government, can have an impact on a range of outcomes, now and in the future.

It is within this school context that day-to-day classroom practice is set, and the following sections focus most closely on the planning that has to take place to ensure that pupil progress at the core.

PLANNING FOR PROGRESS

Planning is one of the most important roles of a classroom teacher. It is the process through which teachers decide when and how to teach an agreed curriculum. New to the classroom, to those in training, it can often seem as if experienced teachers focus on the content of presentation slides or other resources and that, particularly in larger schools where they plan together, adapting lessons for their own class can be a minor part of planning. This can obscure what experienced teachers have learnt over years of planning and teaching, and much of what goes on in their heads when making decisions about what to do before, during and after lessons may not be written down. For the beginning teacher, the process and recording of planning should go hand in hand with thinking about the needs of the children in their class, and they should be planning their pedagogy and assessment as well as the curriculum content.

THE PLANNING PROCESS

For lesson planning to be effective in securing progress for children, the work on creating that carefully sequenced curriculum will have been completed, and the benchmarks and criteria for tracking progress will be in place. Before embarking on the planning process, you will have discussed the relevant policies and frameworks with your mentors and other staff in your placement. You will have made links to your academic studies, and your reading of earlier chapters in this book, and other material. You will understand from this that if the curriculum is carefully sequenced and has the potential for learners to demonstrate mastery at each stage, this represents a framework for progress over time. Your planning will have that curriculum as its foundation; it will structure assessment will be built in at every stage.

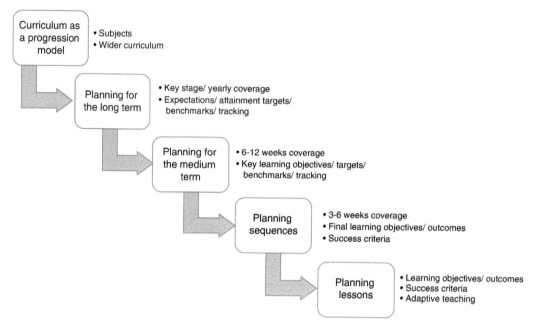

Figure 6.2   Planning for progress: From the curriculum to single lessons

Figure 6.2 outlines an example of a possible planning structure from curriculum to single lessons. Schools may organise or name different stages differently – and use different terminology for outcomes of learning, but broadly, individual lesson plans should come at the end of a planning process that starts with a carefully structured, progression-focussed curriculum, long- and medium-term overviews and sequences or units of single lessons. Early Year teachers will also have continuous provision plans that support and extend direct teaching. Built into it will be the decisions made by the school as shown in Figure 4.2.

The next section of the book uses the headings in the diagram to explore the connections and sequence from the curriculum and long-term plans to single lessons.

PLANNING FOR THE LONG TERM

KEY STAGES 1 AND 2

The published primary curriculum (DfE, 2013c) contains programmes of study set out in key stages: Key Stage 1 (Years 1 and 2) and Key Stage 2 (lower and upper for English, mathematics and science and year groups for science substantive knowledge although this is not statutory), with the English appendices in year groups. The statutory requirement is for the relevant curriculum to be taught by the end of the key stage and the main statutory assessments take place at the end of each stage. Schools will lay out the curriculum content in terms of coverage by each year group.

In the case of the primary curriculum document, the phrase 'attainment targets' is used, but there is no clear indication of what that means beyond, for example, on page 16 at the start of the English programmes of study, 'By the end of each key stage, pupils are expected to know, apply and understand the matters, skills and processes specified in the relevant programme of study'.

Although there is some progressive structure for English, mathematics and science content through the key stages, for foundation subjects' content is split only into Key Stages 1 and 2 and are very less detailed. More of what children should be able to do and understand is contained in the 'purpose of study' and 'aims' sections, and sometimes in preambles, but these are not specific to age. It means that, especially for foundation subjects, we have to think carefully about when we teach parts of the curriculum, and what attainment might look like in the year that it is taught. Attainment of the curriculum content for a child taught it in Year 3 would not be the same as we might expect if they were taught it in Year 6. By closely working with the curriculum, considering matters of progression as well as coverage, it should be possible to frame our key learning objectives in a way which would reflect what progress in each discipline might look like. The identified learning objectives could reflect that curriculum as a progression model.

FOUNDATION STAGE

It is different from the Foundation Stage Framework, where it lays out a series of 'Early Learning Goals' against which children will be assessed. Some are more precise and easily measured than others as might be expected in different areas of the curriculum, for example:

- Say a sound for each letter in the alphabet and at least 10 digraphs;

- Verbally count beyond 20, recognising the pattern of the counting system;

Compared to:

- Demonstrate understanding of what has been read to them by retelling stories and narratives using their own words and recently introduced vocabulary;

- Describe their immediate environment using knowledge from observation, discussion, stories, non-fiction texts and maps.

Teachers are encouraged to use their professional judgement as to whether children have reached the 'expected' level for a child at the end of reception. In practice, schools use the development document to help frame their progression thinking. Development Matters talks about 'observation checkpoints'. To help think about framing progressive assessment statements for reception, it can be helpful to use these to consider how progress might be framed prior to the statutory foundation year, as well as in the reception year. For example:

Around the age of 3, can the child shift from one task to another if you fully obtain their attention, for example, by using their name?

Around the age of 4, is the child using sentences of four to six words – "I want to play with cars" or "What's that thing called?"?

Can the child use sentences joined up with words like 'because', 'or', 'and'? For example: "I like ice cream because it makes my tongue shiver."

Is the child using the future and past tense: "'I am going to the park" and "I went to the shop"?

Can the child answer simple 'why' questions?

(DfE, 2023f p.33)

Even if you are not an Early Years teacher, the areas of learning which are implicit in the primary curriculum but explicit in Early Years (DfE, 2023c) can help us to develop an understanding of progress which can inform our teaching, especially when children are falling behind.

Table 6.1 shows an example of how a series of checkpoints, drawn from Development Matters (DfE, 2023f), might be used to map progress through the reception year.

Table 6.1   Possible checkpoint criteria for reception year

End of preschool/entry to reception	Midway through reception	End of reception
Sometimes plays alongside others Takes part in pretend play (eg, being 'mummy' or 'daddy')	Can identify a range of different feelings	Can say how others are feeling and adjust behaviour appropriately
Takes part in other pretend play with different roles - eg, being the Gruffalo	Can say how others are feeling based on their expressions and actions	Can talk about their own feelings
Can generally resolve conflicts with others during play.	Shows resilience and keeps on trying when finding something difficult	Makes constructive and sustainable relationships with other children and adults
Is developing independence in meeting their own care needs, eg, using the toilet, washing and drying their hands thoroughly	Can say what they are good at and what they would like to improve	Can set themselves goals
	Is starting to sit and listen to adults more consistently when asked to	Can wait for attention
		Can listen to and respond to adults
	Can follow simple instructions	Can follow instructions, including those with two or more parts
	Rarely needs help in meeting their own care needs	Is independent in meeting own care needs

---

REFLECTIVE QUESTIONS

- Looking at the Early Years Foundation Stage (EYFS) framework and Development Matters, can you see where the statements in Table 5.1 have been drawn from? How do they compare with what is used in your school?

- Looking at the tracking document for Year 2 reading, and the English national curriculum for Year 2, can you see how these objectives have been chosen?

- Can you construct some key objectives for Year 3? How useful are key objectives like this in assessing attainment? Would you frame them differently as part of assessing progress?

(Continued)
- How could we use the Ofsted curriculum report for history to help us map the primary history curriculum as a progression model?
- What would our history key objectives be for year groups or key stages?

PLANNING FOR THE MEDIUM TERM

Each year group will have their allotted curriculum content. This can be presented in a number of ways and different terminologies may be used, for example, medium-term plans, curriculum maps, schemes of work and knowledge organisers. They will vary as to content. It is a statutory duty for schools to post curriculum information on their website, so there will always be a range of examples to find on the internet. Some will be detailed not just in terms of coverage but also pedagogical approaches, visits, cross-curricular links, key questions and vocabulary, learning outcomes and resources. They may be more similar to a sequence plan that is closer to actual classroom practice, or in contrast, just a loose outline of curriculum coverage. Depending on the detail in medium-term plans, sequence and single lesson planning can largely be a matter of adapting and refining the medium-term plan to suit the class and the individuals within it; this is more likely to be the case if in larger schools teachers in the same year group plan together, or if there are purchased schemes of work. In effect, these already contain sequences of teaching and learning and show what each single lesson will contain. However, for the individual teacher, planning sequences and single lessons can still be a major part of their planning process. For beginning teachers, it is important to understand the thinking behind any jointly planned materials, or those already in place. They must practise planning themselves, including from scratch, for single lessons and sequences, so they can be ready to plan for progress effectively, no matter the setting or the class. All teachers have to know exactly what they want to happen in each learning episode, and how they fit together as a progressive sequence, whether these are planned in more detail in medium-term plans, sequence or unit plans or in single lessons. The principles will be the same, no matter how these are done, and no matter how much is written down.

Spend some time looking at a few medium-term plans online and thinking about what else teachers would need to do to develop this into a clear plan for a sequence of lessons with a focus on progression, and then look at your own school medium-term plans and consider the reflective questions.

REFLECTIVE QUESTIONS

Looking at the medium-term plans for at least two consecutive year groups for your school, can you identify:

- Coverage of the national curriculum or EYFS?
- How they build on what children already know and understand?
- Explicit content covering the wider curriculum?

(Continued)

(Continued)

- Knowledge, skills or recurring themes?
- Clarity over what the children are going to learn?
- Opportunities for assessment, both through the plan and at the end?

LEARNING SEQUENCES AND SINGLE LESSONS

ESSENTIAL THINKING

A learning sequence is when a number of lessons are planned as a whole, with a key learning outcome at the end. It will develop learning over a period of time, through a number of taught sessions, and in Early Years, well-designed continuous provision to provide opportunities for practice and application. It will have intermediate learning outcomes, designed to contribute to the whole. It is more than simply a number of single lessons taught consecutively. Its focus is on progress through the sequence. As a beginning teacher, you will work with your provider's planning templates, along with the schools. You may be working with purchased schemes, packs of presentation slides and/or sets of non-negotiables made by schools or trusts. However, in any context, the following key questions could usefully be asked here:

- What curriculum am I covering?

  - This will be informed by the long- and medium-term plans in your school or the schemes you are following.

- What do the children already know?

  - Your understanding of this will be based not only on what they have been taught, but what you have learnt from previous experience about possible misconceptions and what you gain from assessment before the sequence, at the start of it and during it. It means your plan must be open to amendments as you go through the sequence.

- What new learning do I want them to achieve?

  - This will be informed by the long- and medium-term plans in your school, and you will need to develop learning intentions, not just for the sequence as a whole but for each single lesson. Your learning intentions must represent progress through the sequence and link directly into the final intended learning.

- How will I help them to get there?

  - This question is at the core of what you plan for you and the children to do during each lesson. The direct teaching and the activities you plan for the children must align with the learning intentions and provide opportunities for assessment, so you can see how they are getting on with their learning and adjust your teaching when necessary.

- How will I know they have got there?

  - Success criteria form the basis of your assessment and relate directly to the learning intentions. They, as the learning intentions, should focus on the progress in learning you want the children to make as they move through the sequence, and the final assessment of their learning at the end. This is a key component in planning for progression.

LEARNING BEHAVIOUR, MOTIVATION AND MENTAL HEALTH

This section looks briefly at a number of other societal and personal contexts which have an impact on learning and progress. Learning is not an unnatural process. We are intrinsically incentivised to learn. We have noted the shift from Early Years from a focus on the 'unique child' and following interests that is deemed possible within a framework of expected outcomes by the end of the reception year, to a more closely structured curriculum based more closely on subject disciplines and the Ofsted exhortation to 'know more and remember more'. One of the problems that may arise when it comes to education, or more specifically schooling, is that what we want children to learn, or what we are bound to help them to learn, is not what they want to learn, or what they feel they need to learn. They may feel they are unable to learn it or fail to see its relevance. What teachers have to do is draw on an intrinsic need to learn, exploit it and plan their interpretation of the curriculum around it. We have already identified motivation as an element in the wider curriculum. We are in an era, particularly through the ITT Core Content (CCF) and Early Career Frameworks (ECF), of using neuroscience to understand more about how we learn, and there is much on memory, and the need to sequence learning so new learning build on prior learning. However, the content on motivation, or the development of learning behaviour, can often be sidelined by the need to 'manage behaviour', and indeed this emphasis seems to be embedded through the title of Teachers' Standard 7. But bear in mind 7.6 and 7.7:

> 7.6 Pupils are motivated by intrinsic factors (related to their identity and values) and extrinsic factors (related to reward).

> 7.7 Pupils' investment in learning is also driven by their prior experiences and perceptions of success and failure.

A good place to start to understand a little more about the impact of motivational factors is Section 5 of a resource produced by Deans for Impact (2015). It identifies these points:

- Pupils should be encouraged to believe they can improve and set their own learning goals; rewards should be focussed on what they are in control of (eg, effort or how they go about a task) rather than ability.

- Self-determined (intrinsic) motivation (values or interest) leads to better long-term outcomes than controlled (extrinsic) motivation.

- Monitoring their own thinking can help pupils identify what they do and do not know, but they might not be very good judge of their own learning.

- Belonging and acceptance are important.

These ideas are based on an understanding of the plasticity of the brain. The word 'ability' can be understood in the moment, or long term:

1. Am I able to do these decimal calculations today because I already understand place value and can follow the steps I need? *or*

2. Am I someone who will eventually be able to understand decimals and use them to calculate accurately?

The second, then, can become a demotivator if we, as teachers, do not help pupils to believe in their own potential to improve, recognise what they do bring to learning and build on it, and do not perpetuate predetermined ideas about how far they can go. If these ideas are in mind as we plan, there will be fewer occasions when we have to 'manage behaviour' because we are more focussed on establishing 'learning behaviours', engagement and investment in learning.

When thinking about motivating children and meeting their needs, we may need to refer to Teachers' Standard 5, Adaptive Teaching. Adaptive Teaching is about all the children in our care. It is about knowing our pupils, their barriers and their strengths and mitigating and using these to aspire that mastery of the curriculum for all of them. As teachers, it is we who need to adjust our practice in light of what we know.

Mental health may not be an area that we think about in young children, or we may not be tuned in to the signs. We may think that it it affects only older children. We do know that poor mental health impedes learning. In 2017, a major survey (NHS Digital, 2018) found that, although the prevalence of mental health problems does increase as children get older, as many as 1 in 10 primary aged children had a mental disorder, and that 1 in 30 met the criteria for two or more disorders. Even in Early Years, a critical time of rapid development, 1 in 18 children were found with at least one disorder.

COVID-19

A good deal of what we hear about the impact of lockdown on school-age children and plans to help them catch up is around curriculum expectations. The funding of a national tutoring programme focussed on English and mathematics is an example of this. Schools are aware that younger children missed out on the important Early Years social and emotional learning, achieved by mixing with other children their age, and experiencing the rules and routines of the school environment. Even with all schools did to maintain progress through the curriculum, children have fallen behind with certain aspects of academic work, and the impact on those labelled 'disadvantaged' fared worse (EEF, 2022). However, there is evidence to suggest that, as the Education Endowment Foundation (EEF) strand on Early Years reports, not only in terms of falling behind in curriculum and social learning the COVID-19 pandemic also affected children's wellbeing and mental health.

The Department of Education (DfE) carried out research exploring the wellbeing of children and young people during 2022 (DfE, 2023f) and seem to have discovered that anxiety and low happiness are increasing, and although their work suggested this is mainly the case with older children, we need to be aware of the potential for the emotional life of all children to negatively impact learning and progress. These, low motivation, or feelings about their own capacity to learn, are areas that we cannot afford to ignore if we want all our children to benefit from the learning experiences we offer. After working through the reflective questions, keep your thoughts in mind as you move on to the next section and read and understand the implications of the principles of Assessment for Learning (AfL).

REFLECTIVE QUESTIONS

How do you think beliefs about ability and rewards can impact on pupil progress?

What can teachers do to encourage motivation to learn?

What one thing could you change about your practice to encourage a stronger motivation to learn, in your whole class, or an individual pupil?

How do you know about the wellbeing in your class, and bow? Are you aware of any particular issues? How are you or your school tackling this issue?

ASSESSMENT FOR PROGRESS

ASSESSMENT FOR LEARNING

We have used the term 'formative assessment' so far in this book, but a lot that has been written about this topic has preferred the term 'Assessment for Learning', or AfL. We referred earlier in the book to The Assessment Research Group. Originally set up in the late 1990s, the group published a set of ten principles which draw together the main ideas (ARG, 2002). They are summarised here:

Assessment for Learning:

- is part of effective learning

- focusses on how students learn

- is central to classroom practice

- is a key professional skill

- is sensitive and constructive

- fosters motivation

- promotes understanding of goals and criteria

- helps learners know how to improve

- develops the capacity for self-assessment

- recognises all educational achievement.

You may see echoes of previous points discussed when we have looked at curriculum, teacher account-ability and development. Notice the emphasis on learning, planning, the learners themselves and the role of the teacher in facilitating AfL. As part of the lesson activity, teachers should plan in those low-stakes assessment opportunities, as well as assessment at the end of each lesson and at the end of the sequence. These assessments are described as low stakes because they do not have the accountability implications for teachers of formal tests and statutory assessments or the benchmarking assessments that the school has devised or purchased. They do not label children as achieving or not, except in the moment. They are designed specially to further learning, to support the teacher, and the child, and to make decisions about what to do next. The outcomes of these assessments should inform subsequent planning and teaching, from lesson to lesson, but should also inform adaptations in the moment and any preteaching or inter-ventions. We can refer to this as an assessment cycle, as seen in Figure 6.3.

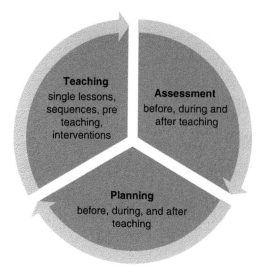

Figure 6.3   The planning, teaching, assessment cycle

WHAT DOES PROGRESS LOOK LIKE?

Consider this quote from Development Matters:

> Practitioners also need to be clear about what they want children to know and be able to do.

(DfE, 2023f p.16)

There are several possible inferences we could draw from that quote, and it takes us back to our under-standing of what learning is. Is that statement arguing that knowing and doing are two distinct sorts of learning, or that learning can, or must, be manifested in demonstrable action? Are we always able to 'see' learning? How can we decide what learning looks like? How can we be confident that children 'know' something? We have already been thinking about this to a degree, when we consider how we will measure children's progress at checkpoints or benchmarks. If the curriculum is right, we will know we have taught a progression curriculum, but how will we know it has been learnt? Decisions have to be made about how the content will be delivered over the year. Built into these decisions will be not only those key learning objectives, benchmarking or check points, but also arrangements for assessment, which may consist of tests, or teacher assessments against sets of criteria. However, the relationship between knowing and doing is not always clear, and a pupil 'product', such as a piece of writing, or marks in a one-off test may not be either valid or reliable evidence of learning that is lasting. The implications for practice in planning for progress is perhaps the hardest concept to get right. We need to consider how we evidence progress, and how we build in assessment processes to planning and teaching at every stage.

LEARNING INTENTIONS AND SUCCESS CRITERIA

Learning intentions and success criteria underpin most assessment cycles, yet sometimes the word 'learning' seems to be lost, and intentions are far more about 'doing' and too focussed on an end product. Shirley Clarke has a broad body of work on formative assessment, including the application of learning objectives, or intentions, and success criteria (2014, 2021).

The key messages (summarised in Figure 6.4) are:

- Learning objectives and success criteria act as a framework for planning, teaching and assessment.

- Objectives or intentions for progress are about learning, not doing. Although Ofsted progress is often talked about in terms of talk about what pupils know, or are able to do, this is not about one task, or the production of a specific outcome; it is about lasting change, what they will be able to do in the future, as a result of their learning.

- The context of the lesson provides the detail of what teacher and pupils will actually be doing and any possible final outcome or product.

- Success criteria, similarly, are about how you will know that learning has taken place. Completion of a single task is not learning. Assessment will incorporate data gathered throughout the lesson as well as at the end, through dialogue, questions, observations and other low-stakes activities.

Tom Sherrington (2021) has written about this last point and other features of lessons described as 'proxies for learning', building on the work of Robert Coe and Dylan Wiliam, one of the original members of the Assessment Reform Group (ARG). Use this website and what you have read so far to help you consider the reflective questions.

REFLECTIVE QUESTIONS

- What have you learnt about the relationship between curriculum, planning, teaching and assessment learning objectives and success criteria after reading this chapter?
- Has anything challenged your thinking about learning objectives and success criteria?

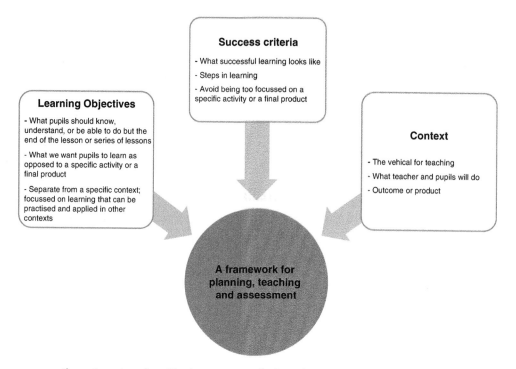

Figure 6.4   Learning objectives, success criteria and context Source: *Adapted from Clarke (2014).*

IDENTIFYING, MEASURING AND EVIDENCING PROGRESS

Moving on from thinking about how lesson objectives and success criteria underpin lesson planning, let's review what we have explored with regard to identifying progress so far. We have reflected on tests and high-stakes assessment that form part of the statutory assessment system and put children into attainment groups. We have considered curriculum and planning in the long and short term and have explored the idea of key learning objectives: a qualitative description of learning and progress through which progress through the curriculum can be monitored. We have been introduced to the idea of low-stakes formative assessment, or AfL, which forms part of a cycle of planning and teaching designed to promote learning and progress through sequences and single lessons. There are three distinct layers, then, of assessment as described fully in McIntosh review (2015). Data may be collected through tests, teacher assessments against criteria or objectives or day-to-day low-stakes assessment pedagogies:

1. Statutory summative (a final goal in core subjects)

    a. Against a national standard (AREs)

        i. Test scores

        ii. Prescribed assessment frameworks and criteria

2. In school summative (benchmarks towards termly or yearly goals in the whole curriculum)

    a. Against a school's curriculum expectations (CREs)

        i. Key learning objectives

    b. A standard generated from widespread participation (AREs)

        i. Purchased tests

    c. Purchased schemes of work

        i. Associated tests

3. In school formative assessment (lesson focussed, day-to-day teacher assessments)

    a. In class assessment

Not fitting neatly into any of these three are assessment opportunities which are likely to be related to accountability, but also, as an independent view, have the potential to inform teachers about progress and inform next steps: learning walks, book looks or scrutinies, discussions with children about their learning by middle or senior managers, for example.

Here we share two extracts from the Ofsted handbook: inspecting the curriculum (2019f).

> They discuss pupils' progress and attainment with leaders to form a view of pupils' outcomes and the means by which they achieve these outcomes.
>
> Work scrutiny will form a part of the evidence we use to judge whether the intended curriculum is being enacted. Do the pupils' books support other evidence that what the school set out to teach has, indeed, been covered? Work scrutinies can provide part of the evidence to show whether pupils know more, remember more and can do more, but only as one component of the deep dive which includes lesson visits and conversations with leaders, teachers and pupils. Coverage is a prerequisite for learning, but simply having covered a part of the curriculum does not in itself indicate that pupils know or remember more. Work scrutinies cannot be used to demonstrate that an individual pupil is working 'at the expected standard' or similar, and it is not valid to attempt to judge an individual pupil's individual progress by comparing books from that pupil at two points in time.

(Ofsted, 2019c pp.2, 9)

What we might glean from these extracts, and from what we have read so far, is that identifying, evidencing and measuring progress is a complex business, and it involves more than simply scores on a test, a completed task or a tick list. Some data may be captured in the moment, and not recorded. Some may be formally recorded against agreed criteria, using one or more assessment activities, and contribute to a summary of progression for individuals or groups of children. Some assessments may tell us very little beyond marks in a test on a particular day or the completion of a task. Learning may be apparent one day and seemingly lost the next when asked to apply it. Some key messages emerge:

1. We all need to agree what we mean by learning, attainment and progress. For progress to happen, assessment will be framed by long- and short-term goals, set against a cohesive, sequenced curriculum.

2. Different assessments have different purposes. We need to acknowledge what they are, and for whom, and recognise in what way they support pupil progress.

3. Assessment tools should be designed to measure what they are intended to measure (validity) and enable us to make consistently accurate judgements (reliability).

4. We must recognise the strengths and limitations of the different forms and tools of assessment and apply them as most appropriate.

5. Lasting learning is unlikely to be demonstrated in a single assessment.

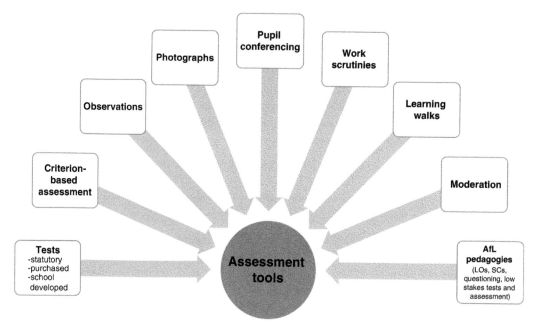

Figure 6.5   Assessment tools

PUPIL PROGRESS MEETINGS AND TARGET SETTING

The last question asks about actions following assessment. Your school is likely to have regular pupil progress meetings (PPMs). These are opportunities for senior and middle leaders to hear about and consider pupil progress, usually referring to outcomes recorded on school tracking documents. Because this is the usual focus of the meeting, discussions tend to revolve about core subjects, and groups of pupils who are not meeting curriculum or age-related expectations, not doing as well as other children in the school or not making progress from their previous achievements. There may be dialogue about what data fed into the judgement entered on the tracking document, especially when test results and teacher assessments do not align. Discussions will explore the barriers to learning of individuals and how adaptive teaching or interventions can be planned to help them move forward.

We have mentioned on several occasions the notion of goal setting, both long and short term. When focussing on progress, rather than attainment, one of the areas that might be discussed during these

PPMs will be progress towards these goals or targets. This is important year to year; we know that expectations have an impact on outcomes, as long as the teaching facilitates that progress to be made. However, we know also that accountability focusses the attention of schools on percentages of children reaching those age-related expectations at the end of key stages, and this will be particularly keenly aimed at Key Stage 2 outcomes. The Primary School Accountability in 2023: technical guide (DfE, 2023g), referring to the government response to the Workload Advisory Group report 'Making Data Work' (DfE, 2019g), makes the following point, focussing on the difference between predictions based on previous attainment and setting goals. The use of flight paths, perhaps more common in secondary schools, is simply mapping progress from one set of data to another, in this case from Key Stage 1 to 2, but often also from reception to Key Stage 1. Thinking back to Part 1, you might notice also the continued use of the term 'level'.

The Government response to the Workload Advisory Group report 'Making Data Work' provides advice to schools about proportionate use of setting predictions or targets for individual pupils to aid teaching. It made clear that predicting pupils' attainment can sometimes be appropriate, but that pupils or their parents need not be routinely told the levels that they 'should' or 'are likely to' achieve at the end of Key Stages 1 or 2. The group also stated that 'flight paths', where pupils are told the levels they will achieve based on the performance data of pupils with similar starting points in previous years are not valid as a prediction, as they understate the variation in pupil trajectories of development. Schools are not held to account by the Department for pupil targets and predictions, and local authorities or academy trusts should not routinely request such information (P28).

David Didau (2019) expands on this on his website. Have a look here, too, before reflecting on the questions.

REFLECTIVE QUESTIONS

Review your school's assessment policy in light of the points above, and the methods of evidencing progress in Figure 6.5, identifying:

- the overall programme of assessment
- the three different sorts of assessment
- long- and short-term goals
- the assessment tools used to measure and record attainment and pupil progress, and their frequency
- opportunities for moderation of judgements, within school and/or within trusts or groups of schools
- what happens after assessments to promote pupil progress?

COMMUNICATING PROGRESS TO PARENTS AND CARERS

The EEF has reported on evidence around parental engagement and its impact on pupil progress (EEF, 2021). This evidence suggests that up to four months additional progress can be achieved and that the benefit is greater for lower achieving children and that engagement become lessened as children get older. Schools may develop a number of strategies to involve parents in their children's education, and the EEF describes some of these. But there are two statutory requirements for schools to make at least two points of contact with regard to pupil progress: to write an annual report and to provide at least one opportunity a year for parents or carers to discuss pupil progress with a teacher. These requirements originate in the 2005 regulations (The Education (Pupil Information) (England) Regulations 2005). Academies, as independent schools, are not required to hold parents evening, but as in most other respects, they will usually follow common practice in maintained schools.

This is the information that annual reports must provide:

- General progress

- Brief particulars of achievements, highlighting strengths and developmental needs

- Attendance record

- The results of national curriculum assessments

This is not detailed guidance. Think back to all you have read so far about pupil progress. Talk to your mentors, colleagues, peers, parents and carers you know. Find out what reports in your setting look like and how parents' consultations are organised. Three key questions underpin decisions about reports and consultation meetings:

What do parents want to know?

How can we meet statutory requirements in a way that is responsive to parents'/carers' wants, and does not represent an undue burden on teacher workload?

How can reports and parent/carer consultations support pupil progress?

PART 4
REFLECTIONS

7
REFLECTIONS AND FINAL THOUGHTS

In exploring the concept of progress within primary education, it is possible to see how important it is at various levels, from the individual level to the institutional level, and at a national level through statutory assessments. In reflecting on the idea of progress, and the role it plays within education, it is vital to be aware of how your cog fits in a much wider and broader machine. This is why we have included some critical perspectives to help deeper your understanding of why 'progress' has become paramount in schools, and educational policy as a whole.

NEOLIBERALISM

Neoliberalism is argued to have a significant influence on perception towards learning, and ultimately what is counted as progress. Harvey offers a useful definition of neoliberalism as:

> *A theory of political economic practices that proposes that human wellbeing can best be advanced by liberating individual entrepreneurial freedoms and skills within an institutional framework characterized by strong private property rights, free markets, and free trade.*

(Harvey, 2005 p.2)

This has led, state Beckmann et al. (2009), to continuous neoliberal reforms which have subjected public services (across the country) to privatisation, marketisation, alternative forms of the 'new managerialism' and, most importantly, the elevation of business management practices in places such as schools. Whitty (1997) argues that the guiding belief behind these reforms has been that the private sector's approach is superior to those traditionally adopted in the public sector. Consequently, public sector institutions operate more like private sector businesses (Beckmann et al., 2009 p.311).

This has created what Ball describes as a neoliberal education system, 'a system animated by personal rights rather than universal values, a system driven and justified by results/outputs rather than any moral principles' (Ball, 2023 p.210).

The emphasis of neoliberalist policies was to create competition between schools to put pressure on them to be more entrepreneurial and maintain pupil numbers. This is because 'choice' was a centre of these neoliberalist policies: similar to being a customer, parents were encouraged to exercise their private choices in which school to send their children, and schools had to 'attract' parents/carers. Sleeter (2009) argues that those who are most affected by social inequality are convinced into thinking that neoliberal education policies provide them with school choice. Instead, neoliberalist policies potentially increase competition for wealth and the shift of public services under private ownership tends to benefit those who are already powerful and wealthy (Harvey, 2005). The children's individual progress that has been measured and quantified through statutory assessments plays a critical role within this system due to the creation of league tables in 1992. The results of these national assessments could provide attainment data to compare not only individual children in their classrooms but also schools as well. This, coupled with school Ofsted inspection reports, meant parents/carers could make informed decision about which school would be best for their child.

The significant assumption behind this 'convenient' method for comparing schools and identifying the causes for that comparison is that it is objective in its approach and that all schools can be studied as an isolated unit of analysis (Wrigley, 2013). In other words, schools are only affected by their inner nature which is changed by the behaviours of staff and particularly the head teacher as 'leader', which overlook the wider forces which can have an impact on schooling and the ways in which injustice is produced and reproduced (Wrigley, 2013).

Ball (2023) claims that this increased emphasis on economic competitiveness over the past 40 years has led to a sidelining of education for social purposes. Historically, social and economic purposes of education have been central to education since the 19th century, but this has substantially shifted with governments reducing the scope of their activities through the handing out of responsibilities to private, charitable or other organisations (Thrupp and Tomlinson, 2005).

INTERNATIONAL COMPETITION

As we examine this further, we come to see how this emphasis on the economy and system of competition has implications for England in the global context. England's economy and standing in international performance league tables are consistently in the media and international comparisons continually drive reform in England (Ball, 2023). Indeed, Ball claims that the Organisation for Economic Co-operation and Development (OECD) is very much aware of the persuasive effects that poor international performance can have on education policy. This is how the OECD, Ball argues, can operate through a form of rational peer pressure towards a range of countries by disseminating 'what works' or suggesting policies that have 'proven' to be successful in countries who performed well in their international performance tests. The OECD's most renown test is the Programme for International Student Assessment (PISA), which has had over 80 participant countries. PISA testing is also considered a major income stream for the OECD, due to the considerable cost for those nations who participate (Ball, 2023). The purpose behind PISA is to provide a global testing infrastructure that compares the performance of nations. It is the educational measurement and comparison of various children on a global scale which have significant implications and influences on national educational policies in England.

PROGRESS FOR SOCIAL JUSTICE

Riddell (2023) asserts that since 2013 there has been an additional emphasis on the attainment outcomes for disadvantaged children. One example of this can be seen in Michael Gove's (2012) comment regarding how our society is profoundly unequal and those who are born poor are more likely to stay poor. This situation he argued led to a 'pointless squandering of our greatest asset – our children' (cited in Ball, 2023). Gove's moral outrage brings together the issue of educational inequality and children being an economic asset for the country under the commitment of social justice. What arguably underpins Gove's concern is the need for schooling to continue to maximise attainment and he places substantial emphasis on this idea of 'human capital'. This perspective interprets children as human assets who, in the future, will provide their (potential) education and skills to the economy (Ball, 2023). This example from Gove illustrates how politically malleable the term 'social justice' is and how this essentially contested phrase can mean all things to all people (Thrupp and Tomlinson, 2005). Dorling (2015) in Riddell (2023) comments on how England has been a country of extremes of social inequality for some time, which have become worse due to the pandemic. Thrupp and Tomlinson do argue how this idealistic term can raise questions regarding the realistic pursuit of socially just education policy, and what that may look like in practice.

One such example which you may have seen is the calls for 'closing the achievement gap' to tackle social exclusion. From a neoliberalist perspective, this is best achieved through the creation of a meritocracy which would enable social mobility. Ball (2023) on the other hand quotes Bernstein's (1970) point that education cannot compensate for society and be able to directly address all social inequalities within society. This is a much broader policy issue which goes beyond education as Ball states:

> It may be that policy makers are looking in the wrong place and educational inequality might be better tackled not inside schools or families but by addressing poverty, and inequalities in health, housing and employment.

> (Ball, 2023 p.162)

This is why, Ball argues, recent policies that aimed to tackle social inequality have, in equal parts, resolved and contributed towards the issue of inequality. This is because, rather than considering the policy itself as a problem, Ball asserts that policymakers instead are quick to blame the supposed policy implementers, for example, schools and teachers, for failing children and students who experience the impact of social inequalities. As teachers, we do need to be mindful that schools and teaching can inadvertently be part of the problem, as these institutions can help reproduce and maintain inequalities, rather than identify and address unequal structures and opportunities.

As beginning teachers, there is a lot to process at various levels of your development. Here we have explored and hopefully helped you to make sense of the statutory frameworks, and the systems and processes adopted by your placement schools, and how these are set within current government policy. We also wanted to briefly explore some critical ideas to help interpret and reflect on the concept of progress; the historical and current national contexts which frame current practice; and the statutory and guidance documents with which you will be constantly exposed to in your career. In these sections, we intended to provide detail to help make sense of the processes going on at a national and institutional level, and how these influence and inform your day-to-day practices in school. We intended to provide you with some tools with which to refine your own practice and support your critical thinking as a teacher. The book is meant as an introduction to new ideas and expose you to critical lenses to help make sense of your experience. Therefore, we do encourage you to further explore these ideas to help inform your thoughts and understanding, to forge your own path as an autonomous and critically informed professional teacher.

REFERENCES

Allen, B (2018) *What if We Cannot Measure Pupil Progress?* Available at: https://rebeccaallen.co.uk/2018/05/23/what-if-we-cannot-measure-pupil-progress/ (Accessed 4th December 2023).

Assessment Reform Group (ARG) (2002) *Assessment for Learning Research-Based Principles to Guide Classroom Practice.* ARG. Available at: https://www.researchgate.net/publication/271849158_Assessment_for_Learning_10_Principles_Research-based_principles_to_guide_classroom_practice_Assessment_for_Learning (Accessed 4th December 2023).

Ball, S. J. (2023) *The Education Debate* (4th ed.). Policy Press: Bristol.

Beckmann, A., Cooper, C. and Hill, D. (2009) "Neoliberalization and managerialization of 'education' in England and Wales – a case for reconstructing education". *Journal for Critical Education Policy Studies,* Vol. 7, (2).

Biesta, G. (2015) "What is education for? On good education, teacher judgement, and educational professionalism". *European Journal of Education*, Vol. 50, (1) pp. 75–87.

Biesta, G. (2017) "Chapter 29 The future of teacher education: Evidence, competence or wisdom?" in M. A. Peters et al. (eds.), *A Companion to Research in Teacher Education.* Springer Nature: Singapore.

Biesta (2019) *Obstinate Education: Reconnecting School and Society.* Koninklijke: Netherlands

Bossard, J. H. S. (1931) "The concept of progress". *Social Forces,* Vol. 10, (1) pp. 5–14.

Cambridge Assessment (online, ND) Opening the door to deeper understanding. Available at: https://www.cambridgeassessment.org.uk/insights/national-curriculum-tim-oates-on-assessment-insights/ (Accessed 4th December 2023).

Cambridge Primary Review Trust (CPRT) (2014) *Response on the consultation on Performance descriptors for use in Key Stage 1 and 2 statutory teacher assessment for 2015/2016.* Available at: https://cprtrust.org.uk/wp-content/uploads/2014/12/CPRTs-response-to-consultation-on-Performance-Descriptors.pdf (Accessed 4th December 2023).

Clarke, S. (2014) *Outstanding Formative Assessment: Culture and Practice.* Hodder Education: London.

Clarke, S. (2021) *Unlocking Learning Intentions and Success Criteria: Shifting from Product to Process across the Disciplines* (Corwin Teaching Essentials). SAGE: Thousand Oaks, CA.

Claxton, G. (2021) *The Future of Teaching and the Myths that Hold it Back.* Routledge: London.

Deans for Impact (2015) *The Science of Learning.* Austin. Available at: https://www.deansforimpact.org/files/assets/thescienceoflearning.pdf (Accessed 4th December 2023).

Department of Education (DfE) (2011a) *The Framework for the National Curriculum.* A Report by the Expert Panel for the National Curriculum Review. Department for Education: London. Available at: https://assets.publishing.service.gov.uk/government/uploads/system/uploads/attachment_data/file/175439/NCR-Expert_Panel_Report.pdf (Accessed 4th December 2023).

Department of Education (DfE) (2011b) *Teachers' Standards.* Available at: https://dera.ioe.ac.uk/id/eprint/13187/1/teachers%20standards%20from%20september%202012.pdf (Accessed 4th December 2023).

Department of Education (DfE) (2013a) *The National Curriculum in England Framework Document for Consultation.* Available at: https://www.bera.ac.uk/bera-in-the-news/new-national-curriculum-for-england (Accessed 4th December 2023).

Department of Education (DfE) (2013b) *The National Curriculum in England Framework Document*. Available at: https://assets.publishing.service.gov.uk/government/uploads/system/uploads/attachment_data/file/381344/Master_final_national_curriculum_28_Nov.pdf (Accessed 4th December 2023).

Department of Education (DfE) (2013c) *National Curriculum in England: Primary Curriculum Key Stages 1 and 2 Framework Document*. DfE: London. Available at: https://assets.publishing.service.gov.uk/media/5a81a9abe5274a2e8ab55319/PRIMARY_national_curriculum.pdf (Accessed 4th December 2023).

Department of Education (DfE) (2013d) *Reform of the National Curriculum in England: Government Response to the Consultation, Conducted February – April 2013*. DfE: London. Available at: https://assets.publishing.service.gov.uk/media/5a7cad46e5274a2f304ef690/Consultation_Summary_Response_NC_v3.pdf (Accessed 4th December 2023).

Department of Education (DfE) (2013e) *Primary Assessment and Accountability under the New National Curriculum*. Available at: https://assets.publishing.service.gov.uk/government/uploads/system/uploads/attachment_data/file/298568/Primary_assessment_and_accountability_under_the_new_curriculum_consultation_document.pdf (Accessed 4th December 2023).

Department of Education (DfE) (2014a) *Performance Descriptors for Use in Key Stage 1 and 2 Statutory Teacher Assessment for 2015/2016*. Available at: https://assets.publishing.service.gov.uk/government/uploads/system/uploads/attachment_data/file/368298/KS1-KS2_Performance_descriptors_consultation.pdf (Accessed 4th December 2023).

Department of Education (DfE) (2014b) *Reforming Assessment and Accountability for Primary Schools*. Government response to consultation on primary school assessment and accountability. Available at: https://assets.publishing.service.gov.uk/government/uploads/system/uploads/attachment_data/file/297595/Primary_Accountability_and_Assessment_Consultation_Response.pdf (Accessed 4th December 2023).

Department of Education (DfE) (2014c) *National Curriculum in England: Framework for Key Stages 1 to 4*. GOV.UK. Available at: https://www.gov.uk/government/publications/national-curriculum-in-england-framework-for-key-stages-1-to-4/the-national-curriculum-in-england-framework-for-key-stages-1-to-4 (Accessed 4th December 2023).

Department of Education (DfE) (2015a) *Performance Descriptors for Key Stage 1 and 2 Statutory Teacher Assessment Government Consultation Response*. Available at: https://assets.publishing.service.gov.uk/government/uploads/system/uploads/attachment_data/file/407178/Performance-descriptors-consultation-government-response.pdf (Accessed 4th December 2023).

Department of Education (DfE) (2015b) *Assessment without Levels Commission Announced*. Available at: https://www.gov.uk/government/news/assessment-without-levels-commission-announced (Accessed 4th December 2023).

Department of Education (DfE) (2015c) *The Commission on Assessment without Levels: Final Report*. Available at: https://www.gov.uk/government/publications/commission-on-assessment-without-levels-final-report (Accessed 4th December 2023).

Department of Education (DfE) (2015d) *Govt Response to the CAWL Report*. Available at: https://www.bl.uk/britishlibrary/~/media/bl/global/social-welfare/pdfs/non-secure/g/o/v/government-response-to-the-commission-on-assessment-without-levels.pdf (Accessed 4th December 2023).

Department of Education (DfE) (2015e) *Interim Teacher Assessment Frameworks at the End of Key Stage 1*. Available at: https://assets.publishing.service.gov.uk/government/uploads/system/uploads/attachment_data/file/461547/Interim_teacher_assessment_frameworks_at_the_end_of_key_stage_1_PDFA.pdf (Accessed 4th December 2023).

Department of Education (DfE) (2015f) *Interim Frameworks for Teacher Assessment at the End of Key Stage 2 in 2016*. Available at https://assets.publishing.service.gov.uk/government/uploads/system/uploads/

attachment_data/file/473675/Interim_teacher_assessment_frameworks_at_the_end_of_key_stage_2_P DFA_V3.pdf (Accessed 4th December 2023).

Department of Education (DfE) (2018a) *Teacher Assessment Frameworks at the End of Key Stage 1 for 2018/19 Onwards*. Available at: https://assets.publishing.service.gov.uk/government/uploads/system/uploads/ attachment_data/file/1125249/2018-19_teacher_assessment_frameworks_at_the_end_of_key_stage_1.pdf (Accessed 4th December 2023).

Department of Education (DfE) (2018b) *Teacher Assessment Frameworks at the End of Key Stage 2 for 2018/19 Onwards*. Available at: https://assets.publishing.service.gov.uk/government/uploads/system/uploads/ attachment_data/file/1119094/2018-19_teacher_assessment_frameworks_at_the_end_of_key_stage_2.pdf (Accessed 4th December 2023).

Department of Education (DfE) (2019a) *Reception Baseline Assessment Framework*. Available at: https:// www.gov.uk/government/publications/reception-baseline-assessment-framework (Accessed 4th December 2023).

Department of Education (DfE) (2019b) *Primary School Performance Tables: 2019*. Available at: https://www. gov.uk/government/statistics/primary-school-performance-tables-2019 (Accessed 4th December 2023).

Department of Education (DfE) (2019c) *ITT Core Content Framework*. Available at: https:// assets.publishing.service.gov.uk/media/6061eb9cd3bf7f5cde260984/ITT_core_content_framework_pdf Crown Copyright (Accessed 4th December 2023).

Department of Education (DfE) (2019d) *Teacher Workload Advisory Group Report Making Data Work and Government Response*. Available at: https://www.gov.uk/government/publications/teacher-workload- advisory-group-report-and-government-response (Accessed 4th December 2023).

Department of Education (DfE) (2019e) *Early Career Framework*. Available at: https://assets. publishing.service.gov.uk/media/60795936d3bf7f400b462d74/Early-Career_Framework_April_2021.pdf (Accessed 4th December 2023).

Department of Education (DfE) (2019f) *Model Appraisal Policy*. Available at: https://assets. publishing.service.gov.uk/media/5c8a576940f0b640d0dc049d/Teacher_appraisal_and_capability- model_policy.pdf (Accessed 4th December 2023).

Department of Education (DfE) (2019g) *Teacher Workload Advisory Group Report and Government Response*. Available at: https://www.gov.uk/government/publications/teacher-workload-advisory-group-report- and-government-response (Accessed 4th December 2023).

Department of Education (DfE) (2022) *Key Stage 2 Attainment (Revised): 2022*. Available at: https://explore- education-statistics.service.gov.uk/find-statistics/key-stage-2-attainment (Accessed 4th December 2023).

Department of Education (DfE) (2023a) *National Professional Qualification for Leading Teaching*. Available at: https://www.gov.uk/guidance/leading-teaching-national-professional-qualification (Accessed 4th December 2023).

Department of Education (DfE) (2023b) *Reception Baseline Assessment*. Available at: https://www.gov.uk/ guidance/reception-baseline-assessment (Accessed 4th December 2023).

Department of Education (DfE) (2023c) *Early Years Foundation Stage (EYFS) Statutory Framework*. DfE: London. Available at: https://assets.publishing.service.gov.uk/government/uploads/system/uploads/attachment_ data/file/1170108/EYFS_framework_from_September_2023.pdf (Accessed 4th December 2023).

Department of Education (DfE) (2023d) *Early Years Foundation Stage Profile 2024 Handbook*. Available at: https://assets.publishing.service.gov.uk/media/65253bc12548ca000dddf050/EYFSP_2024_handbook.pdf (Accessed 4th December 2023).

Department of Education (DfE) (2023e) *Primary School Accountability*. Available at: https://www.gov.uk/ government/publications/primary-school-accountability?utm_source=0715efb7-cb8f-4a23-be34cf824 fa96447&utm_medium=email&utm_campaign=govuk-notifications&utm_content=daily#full-public ation-update-history (Accessed 4th December 2023).

Department of Education (DfE) (2023f) *Development Matters.* Available at: https://www.gov.uk/ government/publications/development-matters–2 (Accessed 4th December 2023).

Department of Education (DfE) (2023g) *Primary School Accountability in 2023: Technical Guide.* Available at: https://assets.publishing.service.gov.uk/government/uploads/system/uploads/attachment_data/file/ 1183466/Primary_school_accountability_2023_technical_guide.pdf (Accessed 4th December 2023).

Department of Education (DfE) (2023h) *State of the Nation 2022: Children and Young People's Wellbeing Research Report February 2023.* Available at: https://assets.publishing.service.gov.uk/government/ uploads/system/uploads/attachment_data/file/1134596/State_of_the_nation_2022_-_children_and_yo ung_people_s_wellbeing.pdf (Accessed 4th December 2023).

Department of Education (DfE) (online, ND) *Assessing Pupil Progress (APP) Assessment Guidelines.* Available at: https://web.archive.org/web/20101007193955/http:/nationalstrategies.standards.dcsf.gov.uk/ node/20683 (Accessed 4th December 2023).

Didau, D. (2019) *How Do We Know Pupils Are Making Progress? Part 1: The Madness of Flight Paths.* Available at: https://learningspy.co.uk/assessment/how-do-we-know-pupils-are-marking-progress-part-1-the- problem-with-flightpaths/ (Accessed 4th December 2023).

Education Endowment Foundation (EEF) (Online, n.d.) *Mastery Learning: High Impact for Low Cost Based on Limited Evidence.* Available at: https://educationendowmentfoundation.org.uk/education-evidence/ teaching-learning-toolkit/mastery-learning/technical-appendix (Accessed 4th December 2023).

Education Endowment Fund (EEF) (2021) *Parental Engagement.* Available at: https://educationen dowmentfoundation.org.uk/education-evidence/teaching-learning-toolkit/parental-engagement (Accessed 4th December 2023).

Education Endowment Fund (EEF) (2022) *Best Evidence on Impact of COVID-19 on Pupil Attainment: Research Examining the Potential Impact of School Closures on the Attainment Gap.* Available at: https:// educationendowmentfoundation.org.uk/guidance-for-teachers/covid-19-resources/best-evidence-on- impact-of-covid-19-on-pupil-attainment (Accessed 4th December 2023).

Find and Check the Performance of Schools and Colleges in England (undated). Available at: https:// www.gov.uk/school-performancetables?ga=2.198756527.1445296318.1575565388-263295034.15688 96104 (Accessed 4th December 2023).

Gee, J. P (2004) *Situated Language and Learning: A Critique of Traditional Schooling.* Routledge: London.

Gibb, N. (2021) *The Importance of a Knowledge-Rich Curriculum.* Department of Education. Available at: https://www.gov.uk/government/speeches/the-importance-of-a-knowledge-rich-curriculum (Accessed 4th December 2023).

Harvey, D. (2005) *A Brief History of Neoliberalism.* Oxford University Press: New York, NY.

Hedger, K. and Jesson, D. (1999) *The Numbers Game: The Use of Assessment Data in Primary Schools Centre for Performance Evaluation and Resource Management.* University of York.

Hirsch, E. D. (1988) *Cultural Literacy: What Every American Needs to Know.* Vintage Books: New York.

HMSO (1988) *Education Reform Act 1988.* Available at: https://www.legislation.gov.uk/ukpga/1988/40/ contents/enacted (Accessed 4th December 2023).

HMSO (1992) *Education (Schools) Act 1992.* Available at: https://www.legislation.gov.uk/ukpga/1992/38/ pdfs/ukpga_19920038_en.pdf (Accessed 4th December 2023).

HMSO (2009) *The Education (School Performance Information) (England) (Amendment) Regulations 2009.* Available at: https://www.legislation.gov.uk/uksi/2009/646/pdfs/uksi_20090646_en.pdf (Accessed 4th December 2023).

House of Commons (2017a) *Education Select Committee. Primary Assessment: 11th Report of Session 2016–17 (5th Special Report)*. Available at: https://publications.parliament.uk/pa/cm201617/cmselect/cmeduc/682/68202.htm (Accessed 4th December 2023).

House of Commons (2017b) *Education Select Committee. Primary Assessment: Government Response to the Committee's Eleventh Report of Session*. Available at: https://publications.parliament.uk/pa/cm201719/cmselect/cmeduc/501/501.pdf (Accessed 4th December 2023).

Majid, N (ed) (2023) *Essential Subject Knowledge for Primary Teaching*. Learning Matters: London.

Martin, M. (2023) *England Placed 4th for Reading in Global Rankings*. TES. Available at: https://www.tes.com/magazine/news/general/england-placed-4th-reading-pirls-global-rankings (Accessed 4th December 2023).

Moore, R. and Young, M. (2001) "The sociology of the curriculum". *British Journal of Sociology of Education*, Vol. 22, (4), pp. 445–461.

Moss, G., Goldstein, H., Hayes, S., Munoz Chereau, B., Sinnott, G. and Stobart, G. (2021) *High Standards, Not High Stakes. BERA Expert Panel on Assessment Report*. Available at: https://www.bera.ac.uk/publication/high-standards-not-high-stakes-an-alternative-to-sats (Accessed 4th December 2023).

National Association of Headteachers (NAHT) (2017) *Report from the Assessment Review Group: Redressing the Balance*. Available at: https://www.ecm-educationconsultants.co.uk/media/1031/assessment-review-group-redressing-the-balance-january-2017.pdf (Accessed 4th December 2023).

NFER (2016) *Understanding Age Related Expectations*. Available at: https://www.youtube.com/watch?v=EIaN6Ko1TnM (Accessed 4th December 2023).

NFER (2018) *Assessment without Levels: Qualitative Research Report*. Available at: https://assets.publishing.service.gov.uk/government/uploads/system/uploads/attachment_data/file/764174/NFER_AWL_report.pdf (Accessed 4th December 2023).

NFER (website) Understanding age related expectations. Available at: https://www.nfer.ac.uk/assessments/understanding-age-related-expectations/ (Accessed 4th December 2023).

NHS Digital (2018). *Mental Health of Children and Young People in England, 2017*. Available at: https://digital.nhs.uk/data-and-information/publications/statistical/mental-health-of-children-and-young-people-in-england/2017/2017 (Accessed 19th January 2024).

Nuthall, G. (2001) *The Cultural Myths and the Realities of Teaching and Learning*. The Jean Herbison Lecture. University of Canterbury December 2001.

OED (online). Oxford University Press: Oxford. Available at: https://www.oed.com/search/dictionary/?scope=Entries&q=progress (Accessed 11th December 2023).

Ofsted (2018) *Inspection – What Are Inspectors Looking at?* Available at: https://educationinspection.blog.gov.uk/2018/04/23/assessment-what-are-inspectors-looking-at/ (Accessed 4th December 2023).

Ofsted (2019a) *Education Inspection Framework*. Available at: https://assets.publishing.service.gov.uk/government/uploads/system/uploads/attachment_data/file/801429/Education_inspection_framework.pdf (Accessed 4th December 2023).

Ofsted (2019b) *Data in the Context of Curriculum*. Available at: https://www.youtube.com/watch?v=zcrp5N6c334&feature=youtu.be (Accessed 4th December 2023).

Ofsted (2019c) *Inspecting the Curriculum*. Available at: https://www.gov.uk/government/publications/inspecting-the-curriculum (Accessed 4th December 2023).

Ofsted (2019d) *Consultation Outcome Education Inspection Framework 2019: Inspecting the Substance of Education*. Available at: https://www.gov.uk/government/consultations/education-inspection-framework-2019-inspecting-the-substance-of-education/education-inspection-framework-2019-inspecting-the-substance-of-education (Accessed 4th December 2023).

Ofsted (2022) *School Monitoring Handbook.* Available at: https://www.gov.uk/government/publications/school-inspection-handbook-eif (Accessed 4th December 2023).

Ofsted (2023a) When will my school be Inspected? Blog June 2023. Available at: https://educationinspection.blog.gov.uk/2023/06/ (Accessed 4th December 2023).

Ofsted (2023b) *Ofsted Inspection Framework.* Available at: https://www.gov.uk/government/publications/education-inspection-framework/education-inspection-framework-for-september-2023 (Accessed 4th December 2023).

Ofsted (2023c) *Ofsted Inspection Handbook.* Available at: https://www.gov.uk/government/publications/school-inspection-handbook-eif (Accessed 4th December 2023).

Ofsted (2023d) *School Inspection Data Summary Report (IDSR) Guide.* Available at: https://www.gov.uk/guidance/school-inspection-data-summary-report-idsr-guide#overview-of-the-ofsted-idsr (Accessed 4th December 2023).

Ofsted (2023e) *Rich Encounters with the Past: History Subject Report.* Available at: https://www.gov.uk/government/publications/subject-report-series-history/rich-encounters-with-the-past-history-subject-report (Accessed 4th December 2023).

Ofsted (2023f) *Getting Our Bearings: Geography Subject Report.* Available at: https://www.gov.uk/government/publications/subject-report-series-geography/getting-our-bearings-geography-subject-report (Accessed 4th December 2023).

Ofsted (2023g) *Research Review Series: Art and Design.* Available at: https://www.gov.uk/government/publications/research-review-series-art-and-design/research-review-series-art-and-design (Accessed 4th December 2023).

Ofsted (online, undated) *About Us.* Available at: https://www.gov.uk/government/organisations/ofsted/about (Accessed 4th December 2023).

Orchard, J and Winch, C (2015) "What training do teachers need?: Why theory is necessary to good teaching". *Impact: Philosophical Perspectives on Education Policy*, (22).

Pembroke, J (2016) Measuring progress. Available at: https://www.youtube.com/watch?v=WtIwr0fQzhI (Accessed 4th December 2023).

Priestley, M and Biesta, G. (2013) *Reinventing the Curriculum: New Trends in Curriculum Policy and Practice.* Bloomsbury: London.

Priestley, M (2016) "Curriculum: Concepts and approaches". *Impact.* Available at: https://my.chartered.college/impact_article/curriculum-concepts-and-approaches/#:~:text=Kelly%20(1999)%20offers%20three%20archetypal,content%20and%20education%20as%20transmission (Accessed 4th December 2023).

Priestley, M. (2019) Curriculum: Concepts and approaches. Professor Mark Priestley's Blog [online]. https://mrpriestley.wordpress.com/2019/01/04/curriculum-concepts-and-approaches/

Pritchard, A. (2018) *Ways of Learning: Learning Theories for the Classroom* (4th ed.). Routledge: London.

Quigley, C. (2022) Cultural capital. Chris Quigley Education [blog]. Available at: https://www.chrisquigley.co.uk/blog/cultural-capital/ (Accessed 4th December 2023).

Richmond, T. and Reagan, E. (2021) *Making Progress: The Future of Assessment and Accountability in Primary Schools.* EDSK. Available at: https://www.edsk.org/publications/making-progress/ (Accessed 4th December 2023).

Riddell, R. (2023) *Schooling in a Democracy.* Policy Press: Bristol.

Selfridge, R. (2019) *Measuring Progress in Education – The Good, the Bad and the Future.* Cambridge University Press & Assessment (Centre for Evaluation & Monitoring) blog [online]. https://www.cem.org/blog/measuring-progress-in-education-the-good-the-bad-and-the-future

Sherrington, T (2021) *Poor Proxies for Learning*. Available at: https://teacherhead.com/2021/07/12/poor-proxies-for-learning-powerful-insights-from-prof-coe/ (Accessed 4th December 2023).

Shipton, E. and Bermingham, R. (2018) *Developing Non-academic Skills POSTNOTE 583 August 2018*. Houses of Parliament. Available at: https://researchbriefings.files.parliament.uk/documents/POST-PN-0583/POST-PN-0583.pdf (Accessed 10th February 2024).

Sleeter, C. (2009) "Equity, democracy, and neoliberal assaults on teacher education". *Teaching and Teacher Education*, Vol. 24, (2008) pp. 1947–1957.

Spielman, A. (2018) Letter to Meg Hillier, Chair of the Public Accounts Committee. Available at: https://assets.publishing.service.gov.uk/media/5bd9608f40f0b6051ce5ded3/HMCI_PAC_letter_311018.pdf (Accessed 4th December 2023).

Standards and Testing Agency (STA) (2017a) *Teacher Assessment Frameworks at the End of Key Stage 2*. Available at: https://www.gov.uk/government/publications/teacher-assessment-frameworks-at-the-end-of-key-stage-2 (Accessed 4th December 2023).

Standards and Testing Agency (STA) (2017b) *Assessment Framework for the Development of the Year 1 Phonics Screening Check*. Available at: https://www.gov.uk/government/publications/assessment-framework-for-the-development-of-the-year-1-phonics-screening-check (Accessed 4th December 2023).

Standards and Testing Agency (STA) (2022) *Multiplication Tables Check*. DfE: London. Available at: https://www.gov.uk/government/collections/multiplication-tables-check (Accessed 4th December 2023).

Standards and Testing Agency (STA) (2023a) *Phonics Screening Check: 2023 Materials*. Available at: https://www.gov.uk/government/publications/phonics-screening-check-2023-materials (Accessed 4th December 2023).

Standards and Testing Agency (STA) (2023b) *Key Stage 1 Non-statutory Teacher Assessment Guidance*. Available at: https://www.gov.uk/government/publications/key-stage-1-teacher-assessment-guidance/key-stage-1-teacher-assessment-guidance (Accessed 4th December 2023).

Standards and Testing Agency STA (2023c) *Information for Parents Assessment Results at the End of Key Stage 2*. Available at: https://www.gov.uk/government/publications/results-at-the-end-of-key-stage-2-information-for-parents/information-for-parents-national-curriculum-assessment-results-at-the-end-of-key-stage-2 (Accessed 4th December 2023).

Standards and Testing Agency (STA) (2023d) *2024 Key Stage 2 Testing and Reporting Arrangements*. Available at: https://www.gov.uk/government/publications/2024-key-stage-2-assessment-and-reporting-arrangements-ara (Accessed 4th December 2023).

Standards and Testing Agency (STA) (Undated) *About Us*. Available at: https://www.gov.uk/government/organisations/standards-and-testing-agency/about (Accessed 4th December 2023).

Teacher Development Agency (2007) *Professional Standards for Teachers in England from September 2007*. Available at: https://webarchive.nationalarchives.gov.uk/ukgwa/20110202175015/http:/www.tda.gov.uk/teacher/developing-career/professional-standards-guidance/downloads.aspx (Accessed 4th December 2023).

The Education (Pupil Information) (England) Regulations 2005 No. 1437. Available at: https://www.legislation.gov.uk/uksi/2005/1437/made (Accessed 4th December 2023).

The School Run (ND) What are age related expectations? Available at: https://www.theschoolrun.com/what-are-age-related-expectations (Accessed 4th December 2023).

Third Space Learning (2020) *The Myth of Expected Progress in Primary Schools*. Available at: https://thirdspacelearning.com/blog/expected-progress-ks1-ks2-life-levels-primary-school/ (Accessed 4th December 2023).

Thrupp, M. and Tomlinson, S. (2005) "Introduction: Education policy, social justice and 'complex hope'". *British Educational Research Journal*, Vol. 31, (5) pp. 549–556.

Whitty, G. (1997) "Marketization, the state, and the re-formation of the teaching profession", in A. H. Halsey et al. (eds.), *Education, Culture and Economy*. Oxford University Press: Oxford, pp. 299–310.

Wood, K. (2011) *Education: The Basics*. Routledge: London.

Wrigley, T. (2013) "Rethinking school effectiveness and improvement: A question of paradigms". *Discourse: Studies in the Cultural Politics of Education*, Vol. 34, (1) pp. 31–47.

Wyse, D. and Bradbury, A. (2022) "Reading wars or reading reconciliation? A critical examination of robust research evidence, curriculum policy and teachers' practices for teaching phonics and reading". *The Review of Education*, Vol. 10, p. e3314. https://doi.org/10.1002/rev3.3314

Wyse, D., Bradbury, A. and Trollope, R. (2022) *Assessment for Children's Learning: A New Future for Primary Education*. The Independent Commission on Assessment in Primary Education (ICAPE).

Wyse, D. (2023a) What works for teaching phonics, reading and writing? IOE Digital blog. Available from https://blogs.ucl.ac.uk/ioe/2023/10/12/what-works-for-teaching-phonics-reading-and-writing/ (Accessed 4th December 2023).

Wyse, D. (2023b) Teaching phonics and reading: PIRLS of wisdom? NEU blog. Available from https://neu.org.uk/latest/blogs/teaching-phonics-and-reading-pirls-wisdom (Accessed 4th December 2023).

Young, M. (2014) "What is a curriculum and what can it do?". *Curriculum Journal*, Vol. 25, (1) pp. 7–13.

Young, M., Lambert, D, Roberts, C. and Roberts, M. (2014) *Knowledge and the Future School: Curriculum and Social Justice*. Bloomsbury Publishing: London.

Young, M. and Muller, J. (2013) "On the powers of powerful knowledge". *Review of Education*, Vol. 1, (3) pp. 229–250.

INDEX